Secrets of a Maltese Girl

A STORY OF POVERTY, RESILIENCE AND THE UNTOLD SECRETS OF A LARGE IMMIGRANT FAMILY

ANTONIA BRIDGETT-TIDYMAN

First published by Ultimate World Publishing 2024
Copyright © 2024 Antonia Bridgett Tidyman

ISBN

Paperback: 978-1-923255-34-0
Ebook: 978-1-923255-35-7

Antonia Bridgett Tidyman has asserted her rights under the Copyright, Designs and Patents Act 1988 to be identified as the author of this work. The information in this book is based on the author's experiences and opinions. The publisher specifically disclaims responsibility for any adverse consequences which may result from use of the information contained herein. Permission to use information has been sought by the author. Any breaches will be rectified in further editions of the book.

All rights reserved. No part of this publication may be reproduced, stored in or introduced into a retrieval system, or transmitted in any form, or by any means (electronic, mechanical, photocopying, recording or otherwise) without the prior written permission of the author. Any person who does any unauthorised act in relation to this publication may be liable to criminal prosecution and civil claims for damages. Enquiries should be made through the publisher.

Cover design: Ultimate World Publishing
Layout and typesetting: Ultimate World Publishing
Editor: Alex Floyd-Douglass

Ultimate World Publishing
Diamond Creek,
Victoria Australia 3089
www.writeabook.com.au

Testimonials

"Antonia's heartfelt story captures her journey as a young girl migrating from Malta to Australia in the 1960's. She poignantly shares the struggles of her large family and the challenges she faced in adapting to a new life, shaped by the expectations of family and society. He experience echoes that of many migrants who arrived in Australia with little but an unyielding will to succeed. Antonia's account is both deeply personal and emotional, offering a profound insight into the lives of European migrants. I found her story truly moving and believe you will too."

- Saro

"From the sundrenched shores of Malta to the vast landscapes of Australia, Antonia's journey is nothing short of inspirational. As a child, she immigrated with her large family, facing numerous challenges in a new land.

This book beautifully captures their struggles, resilience and ultimate triumph in becoming successful Australian citizens.

Antonia offers a heartfelt narrative that resonates with anyone who has faced adversity. Her story is a testament to the strength of the human spirit and the unwavering pursuit of dreams.

Through vivid storytelling, she takes us through the highs and lows of her family's journey, offering insights into the immigrant experience and the power of perseverance.

This book is a must- read for anyone seeking inspiration and understanding of the immigrant journey. Antonia's story is a beacon of hope, showing that one can overcome any obstacle with determination and courage."

- Nick & Shanthi Kugenthiran

"Secrets of a Maltese Girl is well-written, honest and factual.

Antonia's book highlights and explains often unrecognised and overlooked personal struggles experienced by a young immigrant family settling in Australia to make a new, brighter better life.

Describing her family's journey from Malta in the 1960s and beyond. Antonia paints a clear picture of the financial challenges and struggles to keep family unity and values, while making a new home in Australia.

Antonia's story unravels some unmentionable truths, dramas and hardships experienced by her large family, notable her mother.

The book is an engaging and interesting read that will drive a connection with many readers of immigrant background, especially those of the boomer years of the '60s.

For the younger readers, Antonia's story gives insight and appreciation of the struggles and successes of their families when settling in Australia to make it their new home."

- Anna Cuschieri

Contents

Testimonials — 3

Introduction — 7

Dedication — 9

Chapter 1: Growing Up in Malta — 11

Chapter 2: Building Our New House — 25

Chapter 3: Fred's Plan to Migrate to Australia — 27

Chapter 4: The Family's Journey to Australia — 33

Chapter 5: Starting School and Buying Our First Home — 39

Chapter 6: Family Outings — 49

Chapter 7: Mum,s Accident — 53

Chapter 8: Going Back to Malta — 57

Chapter 9: Meeting My Husband — 65

Chapter 10: Starting a Family — 77

Chapter 11: My Big Trip — 93

Chapter 12: More Unwelcome Surprises — 97

Chapter 13: Doris, Health Struggles	105
Chapter 14: Leaving My Husband	111
Chapter 15: Reinventing Myself	117
Chapter 16: My Children	129
Chapter 17: Mum	143
Chapter 18: Travel Bug	157
Chapter 19: Becoming a Grandmother	161
Chapter 20: Doris' Final Battle	177
About the Author	195
Acknowledgements	197

Introduction

This is a story about a family of 15 who were born in Malta and lived in so much poverty who planned to leave their homeland to start a new life in Australia.

How one person's vision and the overwhelming challenge of immigrating to Australia changed life for all of them.

The story details the hardship and poverty whilst living in Malta and the impoverished conditions they endured, and how all family members did their share to survive.

How their tireless six weeks long journey on a ship to Australia begun to start their new life.

This story also explains the challenges they encountered when arriving in Australia, with no idea of the language and how they were welcomed in their new country; having to leave school at an early age and go to work in order to provide for the family.

Secrets of a Maltese Girl

It talks about the difficulty their parents encountered; to control such a large growing family in a country that provided much freedom.

This story talks about what it was like going to school in Australia and the many challenges there were – especially when racism was so prevalent.

It also explains the huge challenges the author experienced when married to an impulsive gambler and losing everything and how reinventing herself gave her financial freedom, where she remarried, was blessed with grandchildren and now lives a life of contentment.

Dedication

To my beautiful grandchildren, Sofia and Isaac, your boundless love and infectious joy are my daily inspirations. You remind me of the beauty and wonder in the world and I dedicate this book to you with all my heart.

To my beloved sister, Doris, who recently passed away, this is for you. Your spirit, love, and memories live on in every page. I carry your heart with me always and your legacy is woven into the fabric of this book.

Chapter 1

Growing Up in Malta

I was born in Malta along with my identical twin, Salvina, and come from a very large family of 13 children: eight boys and five girls.

Mum had a total of 21 pregnancies – complete with a set of fraternal twins and a set of identical twins. She was also pregnant with another set of fraternal twins which she miscarried at five months.

Mum had a girl first and then she gave birth to three boys who died at various ages. One baby died at 12 months old; another died at six months and another at two months. All had various illnesses of the time. I can't imagine what that must have felt like to lose three babies. However, she went on to have another eight boys and four girls.

In between these pregnancies, she miscarried five times. All of my siblings were born at home with the help of a midwife – with the exception of my younger sister Rita who was born in a hospital due to complications.

She breast fed all the babies and I estimated she was breast feeding for over 15 years. Mum also said to us that when she was having one of her many babies, the doctor told her, *"Go and tell your husband to stay away from you as you are not a rabbit and should stop before you get too sick to look after them."*

She told me one day that when she was having one of the babies, she went into labour in the chicken coop and had to crawl on her hands and knees to get out, as her labour was very advanced. When she crawled out of the chicken coop, she called out to my oldest sister Colleen to go and get the midwife. She gave birth to that baby as soon as the midwife arrived. Her biggest baby was 13.5lbs which is 5.9kg. Ouch, that must have hurt!

As you can imagine, Mum would have been an extremely busy women keeping up with feeding, washing and so forth.

There was always someone in the house that was sick with one ailment or another. So needless to say, she was always taking one child or another to the doctors. I remember a time when there were as many as four of us that had the chickenpox at once.

She had no washing machine for washing our clothes and running water. Our source of water came from the well which was in the court yard. We were bathed in a zinc basin, where she had to boil the water on a kerosene cooker.

Growing Up in Malta

We lived in a huge house owned by an English family, and the house was about 300 years old. It was built out of limestone in a square shape with a courtyard in the middle.

My godmother lived upstairs with her husband and family. We lived downstairs below them in an area that was quite big, and another family lived on the opposite side of the house upstairs. We didn't have much to do with that family as they kept to themselves.

In the part of the house we lived in was a huge entry door. On the right hand side was a door that led to a small room which was used for special occasions – like when Mum gave birth to her babies or for anyone that was sick. We were all born in this room, except our youngest and last sibling.

The room had timber furniture with large mirrors and was always set up with clean towels and sheets. The room was spotless – like a hospital room. It was the only decent room in all of our space.

Down a further six steps towards the courtyard was a small room which only consisted of a high table for Mum's kerosene cooker to cook our meals. There were no cupboards for her pots – just some makeshift shelves and no dining room table to eat at. We simply ate wherever we could find a spot.

Next to that room was another room that was just used as storage for the animal feed. Dad cleaned it up and painted the pealing lime wall so they could use for the babies to sleep in. There were no cots just large hammocks in each corner. It was a genius idea as the older siblings would rock the hammocks to put the younger ones to sleep.

Secrets of a Maltese Girl

My oldest brother Fred said that my twin sister and I were always crying and he had to run from one hammock to another to rock us and stop us from crying.

Across from that room, there was another large room where Mum and some of our siblings slept. We didn't have beds to sleep on; Mum would make mattress covers from hessian bags and fill them with hay. I can remember how bad it smelled. And then imagine how uncomfortable it was with multiple children sleeping on the one mattress. We would all be in the middle and on top of each other.

Just next door to that room there was another room where Dad kept his horse he used to work the farm.

There was another big vacant room that we would have to climb 20 more steps to get too. Dad separated the room with a makeshift wall made of wrought iron for the boys to sleep in. My oldest brother Fred said that they would be asleep and often be woken up by fleas and rats climbing over them. You can guess why, as the mattress was made of straw and that was food for them. It was very sad that the boys had to be subjected to such a terrible situation.

Mum and Dad never slept in the same bed but still managed to have that many children – where there is a will there is a way, I guess.

One particular day, my older sister Colleen was changing one of the sibling's nappy while my sister Doris was sitting on the potty. All of a sudden she started leaning sideways, fell off the potty and became unconscious.

Growing Up in Malta

Colleen called the lady upstairs to tell her what had happened as Mum was not home. She quickly came down to watch over my sister Doris while Colleen went to get the doctor. When the doctor came, he took her straight to hospital. They found out she had diphtheria and was in isolation for quite a while. Mum and Dad had to burn all the mattresses and any clothing she came in contact with, and many other items in the room.

Looking back, I'm not surprised this happened as our living conditions were very poor.

As the house was quite big, there were another 15 steps to the roof of the house, above the room where my dad and brothers slept. There, Dad used to breed his beloved canaries; Mum also used to have sundried tomatoes. She used to place them on the rock wall where it was sunny. Goodness know what lurked at night though, as she would leave them there until they were dry enough to eat.

Going back downstairs towards the courtyard, there was another room where we kept our other animals which consisted of chickens for our eggs, goats and sheep for our milk, and rabbits for our stews. We also had almond, olive and prickly pears trees, and of course, our vegetable garden. That was our source of food.

Dad could never have been able to afford to feed us if they had to buy food from the shops. Even though in those days, there weren't too many shops and most people were self-sufficient. Little did we know by today's food standards that we ate very healthy food, as it was all home-grown and with no chemicals. We had no toilet or shower; we just used a bucket and as far as bathing was concerned, we did that once a week in a zinc tub. The same water was used for all those that were bathed on that particular day. Poor Mum had to get the water from the well and warm it up on the small kerosene cooker.

My dad worked in the farm growing vegetables during the day and he also had a night job as a watchmen for the government. Mum used to send us to take lunch to him at the farm sometimes; we were as young as five years of age. Dad never had shoes and he used to make sandals out of car tyres and string.

There were many a times when Mum also went to help him in the farm in between looking after all the children, but that was survival I guess. On many occasions when Mum was at the farm, my brother George would cook a big pot of soup which was our staple food during the week.

After he finished off at the farm during the day, he would go for his second job as a watchmen. He didn't go home to sleep but slept on the floor in the little watch house which was just a very small room. Then he would go back to the farm to start again the next day.

My father did have a hobby, which was folk singing in Maltese. And he would take a couple of the boys with him and also meet some friends there on Sundays.

Fred was often asked by our dad to go to Valletta to pick up any discarded biscuits, bread, lollies and chocolate that people left or dropped on the ground and said he sometimes used to eat the chocolate. This was not for the family's consumption, but for the animals to eat, but every little bit helped.

Growing Up in Malta

Mum roasted peanuts and chestnuts from their trees in the garden for our brothers to sell in the street to help provide for the family. They were as young as five to eight years of age. Some of the others sold vegetables and oranges they had in a wheelbarrow. When the prickly pears were in season, some of the boys would peel them and take them to the city to sell in the school holidays, and they would also pick wild flowers to sell to the affluent people in the village.

My brother Manuel was selling oranges one particular day and experienced something no child should ever have to see. A women ended her life by jumping off a building and landed right in front of him.

Three of my brothers Fred, Frank and Greg, got jobs as bus conductors. It was their job to make sure everyone had a bus ticket and they would punch a hole in it and another conductor would check again when the bus stopped at each location. They started their work day at four o'clock in the morning and finished at 11 at night. What a long day that must have been for them. And the next day, they would do the same routine again. My brothers gave all the money they earned to my father to help with the running of the house and family.

My older sister Colleen got a job working at the local chemist which the ladies from the church organised, while my brother Frank lived with my two aunties who had no children of their own. Because of this, he didn't have to work like the other boys. He still went to the same school as us, but my two aunties would take him for private tuition twice a week as he was very keen to learn and pay for it. When I asked my brothers what they thought of that, they just said,

"It's one child that Mum and Dad don't have to feed and look after." They weren't envious of him at all.

Fred only went to school for a short time as he had a lot of responsibilities put upon him. He was always being pulled here and there to help out. The school asked him not to go back as he had missed a lot of what was being taught. However, he still managed to learn to read and write.

The majority of the boys managed to finish school right up to sixth class. One of them was struggling a lot with school but Mum had no way of knowing as she was so busy all the time.

As for schooling, I have very vague memories and can only remember very little of my education in Malta, and same for my sisters. It is a sad reality that we can't remember a time when it should have been a memorable time of our lives.

The Maltese's were very religious and most of them went to church every day; we were no different. Church was a very big part of our lives. We also went to Sunday school; I don't know why since we were at church every day.

In Siggiewi, we have a festival that celebrates Saint Nicholas: 'Feast Day'. The feast normally last four days in the last week of June. It was something all of us looked forward to going. Mum would dress us up in our best clothes and my father would take us as she didn't enjoy going to the feast. There were many different treats at the festival and my father bought our favourite, which was a nougat that was very sweet.

Growing Up in Malta

The church urgently needed new bells in the north belfry as the old ones had been used for two centuries and lost much of their intonation. A new set of five bells were ordered from England. When they arrived in Malta, they needed to be transported from the wharf. They asked my father if they could use his truck to transport one of the bells. Of course, he agreed.

When Colleen was getting married at a tender age of 17, Mum needed to save some money to pay for her wedding. She was her first child to get married and wanted to give her a nice wedding – just like any mother would. So, she got a job washing the clothes for the army all by hands with the help of Colleen. Fred went to the army training centre which consisted of hundreds of tents lined up in a row. He collected the clothes in an old pram to bring them home to be washed and then returned again.

Mum got the water from the well with a bucket and carried it across the yard. She would say her hands would be red raw from all the scrubbing by the time she had finished. As if she didn't have enough to do! Mum was definitely a determined person and a real goer.

Mum gave Colleen a beautiful wedding and my twin sister Salvina and I were her flower girls at the age of five. Considering how poor we were, she had the most beautiful dress and we had the most gorgeous flower girl dresses.

When all of us children made our first holy communion, we also didn't miss out on having a beautiful dress for the occasion. The girls had the full white gown with tiara, veil, gloves and lovely white shoes, and the boys had the traditional white suits. The only photos we have of ourselves in Malta were taken in a studio when we did our Holy Communion.

Holy Communion of Salvina and I

Mum was also a good knitter and she could knit a jumper overnight. When a jumper got too small for the youngest one, she would unpick it and roll the wool up in a ball and get extra wool and knit a bigger one. That's recycling at its best. You do what you need to do in order to survive – and provide.

Growing Up in Malta

As I said previously, we didn't have a kitchen and Mum used to cook on a kerosene cooker – similar to the type that you would use today for camping. She cooked all meals in one pot which usually consisted of simple meals like soups and stews.

Back then, most families didn't have ovens and if they wanted a baked meal – usually just baked potatoes, onions and aniseed, which was delicious by the way – Mum would take it to the local bakery to be cooked for the price of two pennies.

On Sundays, the streets would be full of mothers taking their prepared dishes to the bakery to be cooked. I can still remember the smell.

When mass finished on Sunday, there were lots of vendors outside of the church selling Maltese pastry called *'Pastizzi'*, a puff pastry filled with ricotta cheese made from goat's milk. Sometimes, Mum would buy some as a treat. We have them here in Australia, too, and now we buy them frozen and always have plenty in our freezer.

There was no such thing as cereal for breakfast in Malta. Mum used to brew a big kettle of coffee and we would dip bread in our cup, and that was our breakfast every day.

As children, we had no toys to play with and so we made our own toys and had our own fun. I remember playing a game called *'Cirku'* which used a wheel of a bicycle. We would take the tyre of the bike and use the rim, bend a piece of wire in an 'L' shape, put it on the bottom of the wheel and push it down the street. We had races to see who can get to the end of the line first.

Years later, I was watching a documentary on the television about Africa, and lo and behold! To my surprise, I saw the children play with the same thing. It brought back such sweet memories. Believe it or not, it was great fun.

The boys played with marbles called *'Bocci'* and the girls played with *'Zibeg'* which were colourful beads. We would make a small hole and try and flick the beads into the hole using our fingers, where the coloured beads all had different values.

Our house wasn't far from the cemetery and whenever there was a funeral, we would follow the horse and cart to the cemetery and watch the burial. No, not a very nice way to pass the time. To this day, there are times where I get flash backs about all the coffins we used to see.

When someone passed away in our village, it was customary for the people in the village to view the bodies to pay their last respect. In those days, they didn't have funeral parlours to keep the bodies in until the burial, so they used to prepare them at home and bury them the following day.

I remember one day coming home from school and my uncle had just died. My brother-in-law used to have the dreaded job of preparing the bodies for the viewing. I got such a shock seeing him in the yard preparing the body. Back then, families didn't consider the effects these scenarios had on young minds. That vision really frightened me and I've never forgotten it. I still think about it from time to time – especially when I go to funerals.

Growing Up in Malta

My mum was always under a lot of pressure rearing so many children. Her patience was very thin, she would sometimes have a terrible temper and her punishment could be very harsh.

My father, on the other hand, was very different and wasn't a disciplinarian at all – as he was never home because he was always working.

When Mum was feeling down or angry, she would mention some things about my father. Because we were so poor, she would often complain how life had turned out for her. We ended up having to struggle a lot financially because my father was illiterate and people took advantage of him. Mum used to say she was always scared every time someone came knocking on the door as they owed a lot of money to a lot of different people.

Mum came from a family of seven girls and one boy. One of her sisters became a nun and the others all married. Her sister Marie and Mum used to work in the farm with my grandfather and he used to say both girls worked very hard just like men. Neither of them went to school, so they spent most of their young life working in the fields until they got married.

Her father (my grandfather) was a very gentle man who always spoke to them with patience and kindness. However, her mother (my grandmother) was a different story. She was a very anxious and nervous person. She had to grow up very quickly as she lost her own mother at a very young age and had to help her father bring up her younger siblings.

Secrets of a Maltese Girl

In those days, she had a lot of responsibilities, so when grandmother had her own children, she took out her frustration out on them – especially Mum. She was very demanding and also had no patience. I have more to say on this a little later in my story.

Chapter 2

Building Our New House

After some time, Mum and Dad decided to build a new home on the land at Blat-il Qamar Road, Siggiewi. There was a big shed on the land that was used to house the pigs that Dad bred for meat and the house was built next to it. My brothers would go there to feed the animals and clean up and sometimes, would sleep there as there was a mezzanine floor in the shed. They would often say there were rats everywhere.

After a long while, the house was finally built, but we still had the animals in the big shed which you could smell from the house. I remember one day going up on the roof of our new house where there were lots of pumpkins that my parents grew. I got the biggest fright of my life when I saw hundreds of rats eating into the pumpkins. It was the most horrifyingly scary thing I had ever seen. Ever since then, I have such a fear of mice and rats, and still do to this day.

We moved into the house before it was completely finished because Mum and Dad ran out of money. They said they borrowed money from my uncle (who was Dad's brother) to finish off the house, so my uncle suggested one of my brother's work for him to pay off the debt. It was decided that my then-seven-year-old brother George would go work for my uncle until the debt was paid.

School in Malta finished at 1:30pm. My uncle would pick him up and take him to the farm. He did that for a number of months. At the time he was working for my uncle; it was winter and it was so cold that my uncle used to carry him in a hessian bag whilst walking to the farm.

Meanwhile, my father got rid of the animals in the shed so that my older sister Colleen could live in it when she got married. Her husband renovated it and they moved into it.

Chapter 3

Fred's Plan to Migrate to Australia

My brother Fred often visited the local bar to meet up with friends. On one particular day while he was entering the bar, a man yelled out, *"Here comes one of the Axisa boys, throw him out!"*

Fred already had a grudge against this man that was much older than him as he knew he had cheated my father in business. A lot of people took advantage of Dad in business back then. Fred woke up to what was happening and he wanted to protect our dad. Fred did a little boxing so he knew how to fight. Yes, you guessed it; they got into a fight and were both kicked out.

Fred went and sat on the church steps with his friend which wasn't too far from the bar he was kicked out from. He saw a newspaper on the ground, picked it up and saw an advertisement for immigration to Australia. He told his friend, *"I'm going to Australia."*

His friend said to him, *"Oh come on Fred, you can't."*

The next day, he jumped on a bus to Valletta to the immigration office. They took his name and other relevant information. He went home to tell Mum and Dad what his intentions were. Dad was happy about it as he had also wanted to migrate to Australia back in the 50s. Mum was not so happy about it, but eventually relented.

So he proceeded to get the appropriate information to apply for his passport. The passport was issued very quickly and within one month, he was on a plane to Australia. He was lucky to go on a plane as most of us came over on a long six-week journey on a ship. He said being on a plane was so exciting and scary at the same time.

Did he know what he was doing or what is going to happen? No he didn't; it was all the unknown.

Even though the immigration department gave him all the information about where he was going, he really had no idea of the enormity of it all. He was only 19 years old at the time and really quite naive to make such a big move. Dad gave him some money which was about £20. When he got on the plane, they showed him where to sit, and he couldn't believe they even had cushions on the floor to put their feet on. That was back in 1964.

Fred's Plan to Migrate to Australia

When he got to Sydney, someone picked him and the other four men that came from the same village and put them on a bus that drove them to the train station. From there, they got on to a train and travelled for three days. They were picked up by a car and driven to a farm at a place called Tully – a small town roughly midway between Cairns and Townsville and had the reputation for being the 'wettest town in Australia'.

The men left them there without saying a word, and after a while, they came back with some meat for them to eat. The men looked at each other not knowing what to do. So, they looked around and found an old wood cabin with an old wood stove. They worked out how to use it, cooked and ate the meat and went to sleep in the little cabin.

The next morning, someone came to take them to the field. They were shown how to put the cut cane onto the train and did that from morning to dusk. They worked very long hours for a couple of months to save up some money – as they figured there was something better out there for them.

Fred and the other four men decided to go into the small town of Tully. There wasn't much there, just some houses a couple of shops and a hall. They went in and saw some men there and with the little English Fred knew, started to speak to them. He showed them the letter he had that was given to him by his girlfriend in Malta. After one of the men read the letter and explained it to him, Fred decided that's where he was going.

He parted ways with his friends and bought a bus ticket to Townsville and a plane ticket to Sydney. What guts he had back then with such little English and not knowing where he was going. He got to Sydney Airport and said it felt so strange and scary. This man who was a taxi driver approached him and asked where he was going, but he couldn't communicate with him well as he had limited English.

Fred pulled out the piece of paper that his girlfriend from Malta had given him, Showed it to the taxi driver who took him to the address, which was in Smithfield, and off on a long drive from the airport they went.

When he finally arrived at the address, there was a man outside. Fred asked him if he was his girlfriend's uncle Mick, and he answered, "Yes."

He invited him into the house and there, he met his wife Katie. They were very welcoming and gave him a room and a bed to sleep in and fed him.

On the Monday, Fred went to where Mick worked in Auburn, which is where they made stoves. He introduced him to the boss and he gave him a job. After a few weeks, they could see he was a very hard worker so they put him in charge in the chroming department. He was always very hungry to learn.

Can you imagine this new 19-year-old immigrant in charge of a small department in such a short time working there? He was learning heaps and then wanted more. So after a while, he left that company and found another job working for *Press Metal Cooperation* in Enfield, producing *Leyland* bus chassis', *Land Rovers*, *Morris* commercial vehicles and *Austin* utilities. It was right up his alley as he always had a love for cars.

As a matter of fact, one day, Fred decided to strip Dad's car in Malta to see how it all worked and Dad was not impressed. He started off as a cleaner at first. After a while, he was asked if he wanted to work in the engineering department. At first, he didn't know what they were talking about. So, they put him in the maintenance section maintaining the spray booth. Fred loved it and learnt a great deal working there – and he was earning pretty good money, too.

Chapter 4

The Family's Journey to Australia

Fred made the decision to try and bring Mum, Dad and the whole family to Australia. He wrote to Mum every week, as back then, the family he lived with didn't have a phone nor did our parents. He explained to her what his intentions were. I was surprised he was writing Mum letters as I wasn't aware that Mum could read because she had no schooling whatsoever.

After a while, both Mum and Dad expressed that they would like to migrate to Australia and so, Fred went to the immigration office to start the process. They informed him that in order to bring us to Australia, he first had to find a place for all of us to live in. So, he started looking for a house big enough for us all. That was not an easy task for him.

Secrets of a Maltese Girl

Eventually, he found a house big enough in Fairfield that was built from fibro and had a wraparound veranda. It had three bedrooms and a big sunroom at the back. So, he decided to rent it – even though he knew he had to pay rent on it until we arrived. He didn't want to take the chance and lose it. He went to a second-hand furniture store and bought bunk beds for all the kids and a double bed for Mum and Dad.

Mum and Dad never slept in that double bed. I still can't make sense of that for the life of me as they somehow produced that many children. He also bought a second-hand lounge and a table setting. He used up most of his wages and had to be extremely careful with his money, as there was not much left for anything else. But he was determined to bring us over.

Mum needed to arrange passports for two of the boys as they were over 16 and had to have their own. The other siblings all had to be on the same passport as Mum, and of course, Dad had to get one, too.

The task to get us to Australia was going well; we all had to have medical examinations to make sure we were healthy enough to travel to Australia and we were all immunised for different diseases.

Mum and Dad didn't have the time to sell their house, so they gave the responsibility to my uncle, who was dad's brother. My oldest sister who was now married with a child was to follow in the coming months.

Finally, it was time to leave Malta and off we went on our six-week long journey on a ship called *Roma*. I was nine years old at the time. There were 13 of us including Mum and Dad.

The Family's Journey to Australia

My older sister came five months later with her husband and baby boy, and of course Fred was already in Australia. Mum and Dad left Malta with only £20 in their wallet. I could not imagine how hard that must have been for them not to have any money while coming to a new and unknown country. They were certainly very brave in those days, but I suppose it was the only option to give us a better life.

We had a cabin right at the bottom of the ship; most of us were seasick and vomiting the whole journey. The seas were so rough we would be walking along the side deck and the water would come over the ship. I don't know how we didn't go overboard. But eventually, we got used to it. I just don't know how Mum could have kept an eye on all of us as it was not a safe place to be amongst all those strange people.

I remember going to the dining room for breakfast and we were served *Cornflakes*. We didn't know what it was and were reluctant to eat it. But once we tasted it, we really liked it. We thought we were kings and queens, sitting there eating all the different food. We had never tasted and eaten such wonderful food before.

After our long journey, we finally arrived in Australia on the November 24 1964. I still remember it vividly; it was one of the best days of my life.

It was a very hot day and Mum made sure we had our best outfits on. She always made sure we had an outfit for special occasions, and that was one of them. When we got out of the ship, there were lots of people everywhere. There was a photographer from the Sydney Morning Herald that must have done some research and found out there was a large family migrating to Australia. He came over to us and took a group photo of us all.

The next day, they had a photo and a story of us in the paper with all our names. That was the start of our lives in Australia. We were met by my brother Fred and the family who he lived with. We were first taken to the lovely family's home for lunch. It was such a hot day and our dresses were made of lace, so they tried to find us something else to wear. They found us some shorts and a top, but we didn't want to put them on as we were so embarrassed. We had never worn shorts before, but we eventually put them on.

When we finished our meal, we were taken to our rented home. It felt right straight away; there were lovely, wide, clean streets – not like Malta where goats and sheep were roaming the streets. I fell in love with it straight away. I can still remember the day we came and how I felt. Coming to Australia was the best decision my Mum and Dad ever made.

We all came to Australia by 'Assisted Passage' – an agreement signed by Australia and Malta.

As I mentioned previously, the task to come to Australia happened very fast and there was no time for my parents to sell the house. My uncle sold it soon after we arrived in Australia, but unfortunately, my parents never saw a penny of it, as he kept all the money. Even though the little money they owed him had already been paid off when my brother worked for my uncle's farm with no pay.

The Family's Journey to Australia

The family's passport photo taken in Malta before they moved to Australia. Top row: Manual, Philippa (Mum), George and Mario; Middle row: Rita, Nick, Joe and Doris; Bottom row: Antonia (me) and Salvina

The day the family arrived in Australia on the dock. Top row: Greg, George, Fred, Frank, Philippa (Mum) and Paul (Dad); Second row: Manual, Mario and Joe; Bottom row: Doris, Rita, Nick, Salvina and Antonia (me).

Chapter 5

Starting School and Buying Our First Home

Since we arrived in Australia late in the year, we didn't start school until the New Year. So, we just spent time settling down in our new home in Australia.

Eventually, the time finally came for me to start school. I felt very nervous about it, although I had learnt a few words in English so I could understand a little. It was a very scary start as we all lined up outside ready for assembly – I had no idea what that was back then. It was overwhelming for me being amongst all those kids in such a big school.

School was very hard as we were treated badly. Unfortunately, racism was rife back then by both teachers and students. There was a lot of name calling that made us feel like second-class citizens and we weren't worthy of being there – which is sad as it was difficult enough being in a strange country (this would not be tolerated today).

There was a lot of teasing from the kids at school as we didn't have proper uniforms and sometimes, we didn't even have proper shoes. Most of our uniforms were attained from the lost property at the school. We were really different and we knew it.

The teachers would put us at the back of the class and we were ignored for most of the time. We only learnt how to speak English through observing the other kids. There were no formal English lessons for us like there is today. You were kept to your own devices; you either sank or swam.

The one's who went to school tried to speak English as much as possible at home. It was a good thing as Mum picked up some of the words too, Dad not so much. I think for someone who had no formal learning, Mum did really well. She actually learnt how to speak and read English – not fluently but enough to get by. She also wrote letters in Maltese to her siblings back in Malta. She was always a very determined person.

For myself, I struggled a lot with maths – for the life of me I just could not grasp it. There was never anyone there that would help me, but I did learn English very quickly and within 12 months, I could read and write English fluently. My twin sister Salvina and I hung around mostly with people who spoke English so we could pick it up from them.

Starting School and Buying Our First Home

I also excelled in textiles as it was hands on and I enjoyed making clothes. My twin sister and I were both very good at sport. We showed a lot of potential on the track and field and in cross country running. The teacher sent a letter home to allow us to train after school, but Mum would not allow it. There was no time for homework or after school activities as we had to help out when we got home from school. Also Mum didn't think that girls needed an education and sometimes, Mum would keep us home from school if she had too much to do.

I was very bitter at the time because I wanted to be just like other kids, and I loved learning. But again, I don't blame Mum for that now, as she had her hands full and am sure she did her best with what she had. Even though Mum never expressed her love to us, I know she loved us in her own way. How could you spread love to so many children with all the hardship she endured?

All the boys except Nick (who was the youngest of the boys and was only just under nine years of age) got jobs within a week after arriving in Australia. Some of them in factories and some in chicken and pig farms. And my father got a job in a factory as a cleaner. My youngest brother Nick only went to year eight in high school. After which, he got a job in the same chicken farm as my other two brothers. This farm belonged to the family my brother Fred rented our house from; hence this is how two of the boys got their first job.

My brother Mario who worked in the pig farm was asked by the farmer to go and get something from the big shed, and when he did, he was confronted with a horrible site of the farmer's wife hanging from the roof. He was so young to witness such a horrendous thing.

Secrets of a Maltese Girl

The boys that started work as soon as we arrived in Australia were only 13 and 14 years old and they never attended high school in Australia – which I think was so unfair for them not to go to high school. I would assume Mum didn't know the law about schooling in this country. But I also believe the system let them down.

They would have had more opportunities in life had they gone to school here in Australia. I have one brother who definitely fell through the cracks and is illiterate – not through any fault of his own – but is very successful in his own way.

My sister Doris only went to school for one year in Australia as when my oldest sister Colleen came from Malta with her husband and toddler son, both got jobs and Mum had to look after him. Mum still had a lot on her plate looking after the household, so she would often have Doris stay home from school to help her look after the toddler.

It got to the point where Doris wasn't going to school at all, and eventually stopped going, but unfortunately the school didn't follow it up. Again, the system let her down. I thought it was so unfair for Doris to have to give up school at such a young age. She missed out on so much and I believe she would have had a lot more confidence in herself throughout her life. My youngest sister Rita was the only one that went to Year 10. Mum tried to make her leave, but she fought her and get her own way. Good on you, Rita.

My twin sister Salvina and I were only 14 and in year eight when we were made to leave school to work full time. We weren't trained for anything special, so luckily, jobs were plentiful then. We got a job at *Amco* sewing jeans and jackets. We had to lie about our age at the interview as you had to be 16 or older to operate a sewing machine.

We worked 40 hours a week and sometimes, we worked overtime. We worked on a quota system which meant that if you sewed over a certain amount, you would get paid extra for any amount over. It was very hard work as the denim was very heavy and we had to lift a bundle of 100 pieces and put them on our lap, over lock them and put them on the opposite side.

We earned AUD$18.20 for 40 hours. We gave AUD$16 of that to mum and kept two dollars. We were very frugal and believe it or not, we actually saved some of it. Dad drove us to work and Mum bought all the necessary things we needed. We lived very simply, and any clothes we had, we looked after them. Most of the time, we bought them from the second hand store anyway.

Mum looked after all the money here in Australia and the family members that had jobs gave all their wages to her. She was extremely good with money and knew how to shop and save. Even though everyone who worked gave their pay to her, she bought whatever was needed for the family and home – from clothes to toiletries and whatever else they needed.

You can imagine what it would take to feed all of us. Mum went shopping practically every day; she would walk to the shops with one of those buggies on wheels. She would buy around six loaves of bread a day and kilos of meat and a lot of cheeses and cold meats for lunches. We also had a vegetable garden, so she didn't have to buy too many vegetables. She would wait for us girls to come home from school so we could start peeling the many veggies for our meal.

Mum always cooked soup first and then a meat dish. This only happened since we came to Australia as for some reason, a few of my brothers became very fussy eaters. The boys had big appetites, so Mum always had to have plenty of food prepared. She had a full time job just keeping up with the meals alone.

By the time we were in Australia for one year, my parents saved enough money with the help of my brothers for a deposit on our first home – which was also in Fairfield, not far from the shopping centre and schools. It was good for Mum as she didn't drive and had to walk everywhere. Even if she did take a bus, she could never carry all the groceries on the bus as she had always had a full trolley.

The house had four very big bedrooms; one with a really big built-in wardrobe and another two built-in wardrobes in both hallways. We had one bathroom, a lounge, a separate kitchen and a large dining room. There was also a sun room at the back with an attached laundry and toilet. At least we had two toilets.

Unfortunately, we only had cold water. The house was built by another large Maltese family. It was built of double bricks had multiple sheds on the land – the land was huge. The sheds at the back of the block were used for chickens and rabbits that Mum and Dad bred for our meals.

Mum managed to buy all the necessary furniture that was needed as this was a bigger home. What she couldn't buy in cash, she put it on

Starting School and Buying Our First Home

three months interest-free and made sure she paid them off before the three months were due. I used to watch her sort out the money and put the different amounts in paper bags for payment. When I got older, I followed the same process – except I used envelopes instead of paper bags.

A day or so after we moved into our new home, Mum decided to do some washing. As soon as she turned on the power, she was electrocuted. She started screaming and Dad went to help her and he was also electrocuted. If it wasn't for the quick thinking of one of my brothers, they wouldn't be alive today. Somehow, he grabbed something and turned off the power point. It was so frightening to see both my parents being electrocuted.

We were all getting on with our lives as best as we could, however, the girls and Mum had to get up at 4am every day to prepare lunches for our brothers to take to work. And as always, coffee was ready for them when they woke up.

After they left for work, we would make all their beds – which was not easy as there were top and bottom bunks. It was the only way everyone could fit in the rooms. I guess it was the girls turn, as the boys worked at a very young age to provide and now we had to do our bit.

My sister and her husband were also living in our house and both worked full time, so we would make her bed as well. By the time we did all that, we had no time to eat anything and were always late for school, which we often got in trouble for.

Secrets of a Maltese Girl

The girls all had their jobs to do. My sister Doris was in charge of cleaning the kitchen, dining room and bathroom, my younger sister Rita had to keep the lounge room and family room clean. And my twin sister Salvina and I had to look after all the bedrooms. Mum did all the cooking and the washing of clothes. We didn't argue like kids do today – we just did it, as it was expected of us.

By the time I was around 12 or 13 years of age, my twin sister and I worked in a chicken farm on weekends (where my brothers worked) to help financially. We collected eggs from the cages and fill up the baskets. We had a basket on each arm and carried them to the shed for the eggs to be sorted into sizes. The basket was so heavy that the veins on my neck felt like they were going to pop out. I was always so scared because there were so many rats, and we both had a phobia of them – and still do.

Because we worked at the chicken farm, Mum got another great idea of selling eggs to people we knew. Once I had to take a dozen eggs to this lady who lived about 2km away. I had to go there by bike, and it was such a hot day. As my bike didn't have good brakes, I tried to stop the bike with my foot, it got stuck in the wheel and over I went.

It took me a while to get walking again as I injured my ankle really bad. So I hopped along the rest of the way with most of the eggs broken. I knocked on the door crying as I was in a lot of pain and the lady let me in and offered me a cup of tea and said it would settle me down.

I left her place and pushed the bike home because it was damaged and couldn't be ridden. I knew I would be in big trouble when I got

Starting School and Buying Our First Home

home, and sure enough, Mum screamed at me and made me go back again with the next lot of eggs for the same lady with a different bike. The poor lady couldn't believe that Mum had made me go back again. Mum was tough but she had to be.

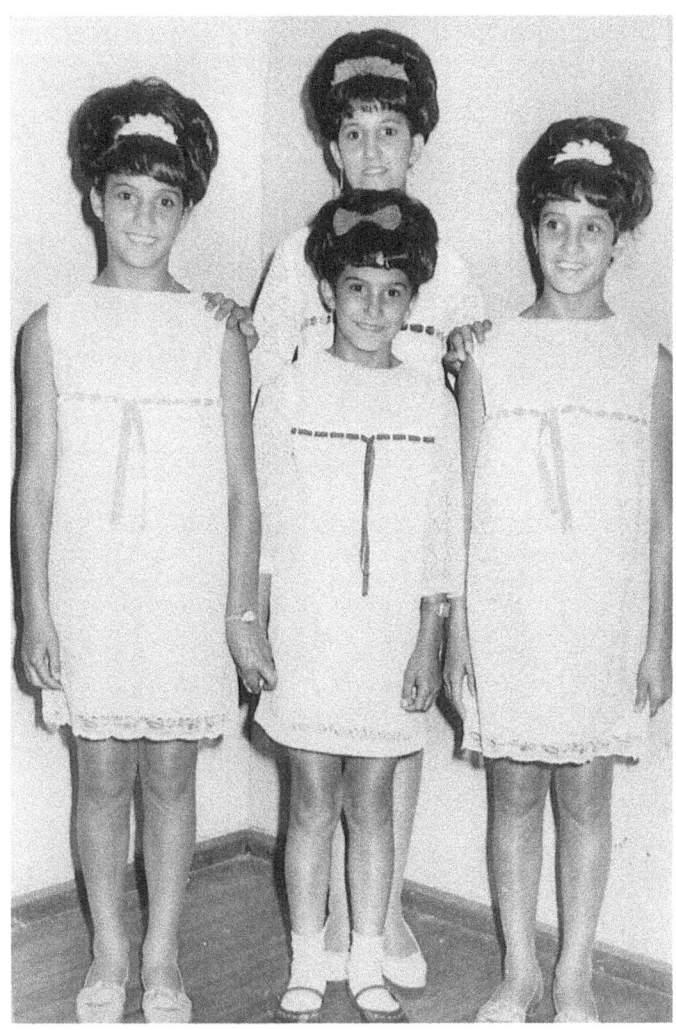

Antonia and her sisters dressed up for a wedding in Australia. Left to right: Salvina, Doris, Rita and Antonia (me).

Chapter 6

Family Outings

My brother Greg loved fishing, so my parents decided to buy a boat for everyone to share. Most of the time in the warmer months, we all went fishing nearly every weekend. We went to places like Brighton-Le-Sands, San Souci, and our favourite place, Neilson Park, which was in the North Shore. There would be at least 11 of us wedged into a *Holden* station wagon.

In those days, you didn't have to wear seat belts. Mum and the girls would get up very early in the morning to cook lunch. It wasn't just bread and cold meats. It was a full on lunch, a lot of bread and watermelons and of course, flasks of hot coffee.

She would take food in saucepans and then heat them up on a primus stove. Most of the beaches we went to had big parks around them and we always got a spot under a tree as Mum didn't swim and needed some shade. We would collect discarded glass bottles on the beach, take them to the shop, get money for them and buy ice cream with it. We got a lot of strange looks from the people on the beach. But it's still one of my favourite memories.

This particular beach, Nielson Park, was the beach I nearly drowned in. My sister-in-law's sister took me in the water with a float, but the float got away from us and I started to sink as I didn't know how to swim. It's true what they say about seeing stars when you are drowning, as I certainly did. All I can remember after that was lying on the beach with people all around me. I must have been saved by a lifesaver on duty.

Mum had no idea what happened; we were too scared to tell her in case I got into trouble.

The other thing we did as a family was going rabbit hunting. Dad used to make these nets for the rabbits to go into. He had ferrets and he would put down a rabbit hole and the ferrets would force the rabbit to come out into the net. We also visited friends that Mum made when we were making our way to Australia on the ship. I think Mum enjoyed that as she didn't have to prepare anything, and it was a bit of a break for her.

Three of my brothers Manual, Frank and Joe started boxing. Mum didn't like it at all as she was put under more pressure to cook special food for them because they were in serious training. So again, life became more stressful for her – and in turn, for us.

Family Outings

By now, the boys were into boxing in a big way, so my parents decided to build a big garage for them so they could put a boxing ring in it. The garage was so big you could fit 10 cars in it. It really was a very big block of land.

I guess all the training paid off for the boys, as Manual tried out for the *Olympic trials* and came third in the Flyweight division. He was also the runner up for L/Flyweight and won the *Golden Gloves Award*. And my other brother Joe won the State title in the Lightweight division.

Chapter 7

Mum's Accident

Growing up, we were always keeping the house going by cleaning or helping Mum cook, shop and iron. Back then, Mum used to boil our white laundry in caustic soda in a big pot to get them bright again.

One morning, she put the kerosene cooker on the old boiler that didn't work anymore in the laundry. She was looking after my second nephew at the time, and he was in a pram not far from the boiler.

While she was stirring the whites, the cooker slipped and the pot fell on top of her, burning 50% of her body. It just missed my nephew that was only two months old. She started screaming really loud and the siblings that were there were all in shock when we saw her. We automatically went to get the hose to hose her down.

One of the boys thought quickly and striped her clothes off and wrapped her in a blanket. I can still remember it like it was yesterday. Her skin was literally falling off, as you can imagine the damage the caustic soda caused.

They drove her to Fairfield Hospital and they kept her waiting in agony for quite a long while. When they finally saw her, they did what they had to do, and she was wrapped up like a mummy.

After many days in hospital, she was sent home to recuperate. She had been home for quite a while and hadn't had her bandages changed, so one of the boys took her back to the hospital. She was already starting to smell and they just got her in time before it started to go gangrene. She was in so much pain. And Mum still had to look after my nephew. Thank god my sister Doris was there to help out.

Mum did get better after a long time, but her scars were horrendous. The skin on both her arms had melted and her stomach was burnt, as well as part of her legs. When she needed to have blood tests done, it was very difficult for the doctors to find a vein. But she soldiered on like a trooper, being the tough women that she was.

One day, Mum was having one of the many arguments with one of the boys about something, and he got really angry and put his fist through a glass door, slicing his hand open. There was blood everywhere and another brother took him to hospital to get it stitched. These arguments were happening more frequently and both Mum and the girls became quite frightened, as the boys were becoming more and more demanding in many ways.

Mum,s Accident

Mum could see what was happening but could not do anything about it, and Dad never disciplined the boys either – so, Mum took all the brunt.

Mum couldn't stand the stress of what was happening and how it was affecting the family. She bought us all to Australia so we could live a better life, but all she really got was more worries. I guess having a large family brings many challenges and there was always something happening with someone. So, Mum had had enough and decided to end her life.

She took a whole lot of pills and was asleep in the lounge room for a long time. She didn't go in there much, and we thought it was strange that she did. One of the boys knew there was something strange about it, too. So he asked us, *"How long has Mum been in there?"*

And we said, *"About two days."*

He tried to wake her up but couldn't, so he took her to the hospital. They pumped her stomach and sent her to Rydalmere Hospital where she was admitted to the mental ward. She wasn't crazy, but just exhausted. It was so sad to see her there, but she needed help.

There were some really troubled people there. I can't remember how long she was in there for, but she would help with the cleaning just to pass the days.

After quite a while, she was discharged and we all tried to get on with our lives as best as we could.

Some of the boys had girlfriends and were planning to marry, but Mum was obviously still very troubled as I used to hear her crying all the time. Many a night I would be awakened by her cries. It got so bad that I couldn't sleep as I was lying there, waiting for the crying to start.

Chapter 8

Going Back to Malta

Mum was still very unsettled and she didn't want us exposed to the things the boys got up to. Mum used to get all us girls in the front room of the house and we would say the rosary every night.

One day, Mum told Dad that she wanted to go back to Malta as she wasn't coping and had enough. We had been in Australia for just under six years, so it was decided that we go back. Some of the boys didn't want to go back to Malta – especially the ones who had girlfriends which was understandable.

Fred found a house in Canley Vale for himself, Joe and Greg to live in – while others lived in their girlfriend's parent's granny flats. In those days, a lot of people converted their garages into granny flats.

Mum started to organise the move and get passports again – we were still to be on Mum's passport as we were all under the age of 18.

It was decided that the youngest girls – me, Doris, Salvina and Rita – and my youngest brother Nick and Mum would go first, and Dad was to stay back and sell the house. We couldn't afford to fly there, so we again had the six-week long journey by ship.

I was not looking forward to it as I remembered how sick we all were when we first came to Australia. I left work and felt sad to be leaving Australia. We boarded the ship and proceeded on our journey back home to Malta.

Again we were seasick, but not as bad as the first time. We had a fairly good time on the ship as we were older then; I was nearly 16. We played a lot of bingo and Mum enjoyed it too – she seemed a little more relaxed.

We finally got to Malta and we were met by some of our aunties, uncles and cousins. It felt really strange to see them all again as six years was a long time for a young person to be away from the country they were born in and the people they knew.

We stayed at our Dad's sister's house and because the houses are made of limestone and it was winter, it was extremely cold. They had no heating which was very hard on us as were used to heating in Australia. We hated it and we cried for the first week and wanted to go back to Australia.

Going Back to Malta

They had taps and a toilet by then, but no hot water or showers. So we used to go to our cousins place to have a shower there. Mum was always thinking ahead, so she started to buy some furniture for us – mostly beds and wardrobes for our clothes. I can still remember where she bought them from. It was from a village called Humrun.

Within a week, a crate full of our things from Australia arrived and we emptied it and got settled in a little more. It took us around two weeks to get used to Malta again; it helped having our cousins to hang around with. We would do everything together, so it felt like home again.

Mum started asking around regarding job prospects for us, and the only jobs available for us girls were as housemaids. I don't know what jobs she thought there was for us as we had no degrees or much education.

Mum felt very disheartened as she felt there was no future in Malta for us. She didn't want us to be housemaids and said, *"I took you away from that six years ago."*

She wanted a better life for us, so she decided that we should go back to Australia – only after we had been there for a couple of weeks. She sent a telegram to our father to let him know things haven't changed much in Malta and that we were coming back and not to sell the house.

Well, you wouldn't believe it – but he had just sold the house and couldn't get out of it. So, he was to stay in Australia as we were coming back anyway.

In the meantime, she asked him and the boys to start looking for another house to buy in the Fairfield area. Again, she goes off to Valletta to start organising our journey back home. We just unpacked all our belongings the day before she made up her mind to come back. She booked the ship back to Australia and we were to leave Malta in four weeks' time.

Again another six-week journey on a ship. We were becoming season travellers at this point! We had the daunting task to start unpacking again and put our belongings back into the same crate we had when we arrived back in Malta. She left most of the furniture there for our aunties to sell.

When it got closer to the time we had to leave, we didn't want to go as Malta had started to feel like home again. I think it was because we were older and had more independence.

The day came to leave Malta again and we said our goodbyes and went off to board our ship once again and hopefully, for the last time. When you think about it, we spent six weeks on the ship to go to Malta and another six weeks was spent in Malta and six weeks back to Australia. That was a lot for Mum to handle. I think she was so amazing to take on such a huge responsibility on her own. Talk about resilience.

This time we had a lot of fun on the ship. Again, we played a lot of bingo and participated in other activities. We went to dances and celebrated New Year's Eve. My twin sister and I celebrated our 16th birthday. All and all, it was a fun, eventful time.

Going Back to Malta

We arrived back in Australia and again, it was a very hot day as it was summer time. We went to live in my sister's garage for a while until my parents bought another house.

They found another house just across the lane way from my sister's place. It was a new house and nearly completed and had three bedrooms, a lounge, combined kitchen and dining room, one bathroom and a laundry room with a toilet in it – and a double garage.

I thought they were lucky to find that house close to the shopping centre and not far from my older sister. We moved into that house a couple of months after we arrived. This time, it wasn't as crowded as we only had three boys, four girls and my parents.

My twin sister and I got our old job back at *Amco*, and we both decided to do a typing course to try and get a better job in the future. We both enjoyed it and were doing well and feeling good at the prospect of getting a better job at some stage.

We weren't allowed to go out much, but when I was around 17, one of my brothers introduced me to this boy and took me to meet him. We were in the car and he started to kiss me which was a big shock to me as I had never kissed a boy before. I thought it was horrible and told my brother I didn't like him.

In the summer time, my sisters and I would go to the public pool in Cabramatta. Mum wouldn't allow us to wear a bikini. It had to be a full swimming costume and we always had to buy them from the second hand shop. We were teenagers and my twin sister and I wanted to look good just like every other teenager. So, we defied

Secrets of a Maltese Girl

Mum and went to this place at Fairfield and bought ourselves a mustard-colour bikini. We thought we looked great and tried to hide it from Mum by washing it ourselves.

I met this other boy at the pools who I saw secretly for a little while. Once winter came, we no longer went to the pool, so I didn't see him again.

We didn't go to pubs or movies like most teenagers did. Mum would never allow it. I joined a netball team which I loved and was good at it. Because I was a good runner, they put me in centre. I had to walk and make my own way there, which took me close to one hour– so I often went early to rest before the game. I did that for a few years and enjoyed it so much.

The factory I was working at wasn't doing so well – even though it was one of the biggest manufacturer of jeans, and I was made redundant. By this time, I had some typing skills and got myself a job in a paint factory in the office.

It was a bit far, but Dad worked in the same suburb and he drove me there and picked me up. I really didn't enjoy it all that much as even though they said they would train me in the office, most of the time I was on the factory floor. I only worked there for a year or so.

Going Back to Malta

Rita, Doris, Nick, Philippa (Mum), Salvina and Antonia (me) on our way back from Malta for the second time.

Chapter 9

Meeting My Husband

At Christmas time, we went on our normal camping site up the Central Coast. We had one of those army tents, as we needed a big tent for our large family. One of our favourite swimming spots was the rock pool at Norah Head.

My sisters and I were swimming this particular day when this young man came over and started talking to me and we seemed to hit it off. I kind of liked him straight away as I was impressed anyone had shown interest in me.

His name was Vic, he was also Maltese but much older than me by nine years. I was nearly 18 and he was 27. It was common in those days that the man was much older than the women. He asked me where we were camping and I tried to explain it to him the best way

I could. He came around our tent to see me the next day, met Mum and off we went to the pool with my twin sister in tow. He said he only decided to come up the coast on the spur of the moment and that he hitch-hiked up. That should have been a warning sign, but I was very young and naive.

By the time I left to go back home, we had built up a bit of a friendship. He asked me for my address and he came to see me at home and met Mum again. Mum knew a little about his family. Vic had come to Australia with his family when he was three years old.

His father came first to set up home and bought a block of land at Smithfield. He couldn't afford to build a house, so he pitched a tent on the land. The rest of the family followed, and they had another child. When my brother Fred first came to Australia, he knew of them as they lived across the road from his family.

Two or so years after they arrived, his father decided to build a home on the block of land, and just before it was completed, his Mum died who had been five months pregnant at the time.

Life became extremely hard and difficult for them after their mother died. Vic's father had to bring up four of the younger ones, as the other siblings were already married. He looked after them as best he could, and he used to take the youngest daughter of 18 months to work with him in a box, and the ladies at work would look after her for him.

After a while, he couldn't cope, so he decided to put Vic and his two younger siblings in an orphanage. Vic had a very hard time in there and didn't have a nice word to say about it. From what he said, they were very cruel and treated them badly.

His father took them out of the orphanage when he could and would move house all the time, so the kids didn't have stability. Sometimes, he would move them from one state to another.

Vic said to me one day that his father got so desperate, trying to work, and look after the family. He was constantly taking them in and out of the orphanage. He didn't know where to turn. So one day, he took the three younger ones to Watsons Bay where he was going to throw them and himself of the cliffs into the ocean to end it all. How very sad to have to make such a drastic decision. Luckily, he didn't go through with it.

Considering Vic went to 13 different schools, he did okay. From what he used to say, he was a bit of joker, always looking for attention.

For some strange reason, their father took them to New Zealand to live. After a while, his father needed to come back for his older son's wedding, so Vic and his younger brother decided to stay there for a couple of years.

Vic and I weren't allowed to go out on our own; one of my siblings had to come with us. Our courtship was mostly at home when he visited me, and on the odd occasion, we would go to the movies. The relationship started to get serious, and it was expected by our parents that you didn't go out with a boy just for fun, but with the intention to get married. He didn't have a car, hence why he hitch-hiked up the coast.

He was living with his younger married sister at the time who had three children which he helped look after. I asked him why he didn't have a car and he said he couldn't afford it. Again, that should have been another red flag.

If I was to marry Vic, I needed to teach him how to save his money so we could plan for the future because he had no savings at all – which I thought was strange. After all, he didn't have a mortgage, car payments or high rent to pay, so why didn't he have some money saved up? We discussed it and it was decided that I'd take control of the money. He gave me his pay which was cash in those days, and I would give him enough money to live on for the week.

It only took us six months to save the money to buy a car and own it outright. I was still giving Mum most of my earnings. And since we were planning to marry, Mum said I didn't have to give her all of my pay, as I needed to start saving seriously. We continued to save as much money as we could. We got engaged in October, just 10 months after we met and set the wedding date for September the following year. We had an engagement party at home which was lovely and then proceeded to plan the wedding.

Mum had done the planning thing a few times as some of my brothers were married and my twin sister married the year before. I was to wear the same wedding dress as my sister. As a matter of fact, all four sisters wore the same dress but had different head pieces. Two of my sisters were a little taller, so we just added to the bottom of the dress. It still looked very nice and you couldn't see the difference.

Meeting My Husband

Vic and I continued to work hard to save money to buy a house. I was so frugal with money; I would walk instead of catching a bus – just to save five cents.

And there was no such thing as eating out or even having a coffee while I was out shopping. If I felt like a coffee, I waited until I got home. The lunches for work were always made at home and on the very rare occasion, I would buy a cream bun for morning tea as they were my favourite cakes.

About four months before we were to get married, we had a little saved up so I suggested to Vic that we could buy a house, as between us we had enough money for a deposit. By then, he was doing really well with his savings as he continued to give me his pay and I would put it in the bank for him.

He worked all the overtime that was offered to him and was earning pretty good money. He had around AUD$2,500 which was quite an achievement in such a short period of time. I had around AUD$1,500 saved up as I also worked all the overtime that was offered to me and worked even harder with the bonus system we had. He knew where the bank account was, so he had access to it if he wanted to.

Back then, you could buy a house for around AUD$13,000. Not a new house, just a three bedroom house but more than enough for us. He kept ignoring my suggestion and I kept harping on about it. When I questioned him as to why he didn't want to buy a house yet, he was very quiet, so I pursued it further and that's when he told me he'd gambled all the money I had put in the account for him. I was shocked as I wasn't aware he was gambling.

I had heard he used to gamble before, hence why he had nothing. I didn't know much about gambling as I was never exposed to it. None of my brothers gambled so I wasn't aware of the signs to look for. He had gambled all the money he had in the account, over AUD$2,500 which was a lot of money in those days – a rough equivalent of AUD$10,000 in today's standards. Thank goodness he didn't have access to my account. At least we had some money.

By then, all the wedding arrangements were organised, and I just didn't know what to do. If I should continue the relationship or go ahead with the wedding. I didn't want to tell Mum about it as I have seen Mum tackle so many problems with the family and didn't want to burden her with mine.

I remember going to work and crying uncontrollably. My work colleagues would ask what was wrong and I just couldn't tell them as I was too embarrassed about it. I was tormented with the decision I had to make and cried for days. I was only a little over 19 years of age at the time.

After a lot of thought and sleepless nights, I told Mum what had happened but she didn't have much to say about it and was sure she wanted me to go ahead with the wedding. If I didn't, I would have felt like I'd disgraced the family. So I had made the decision to go ahead with the wedding.

Vic and I had a big discussion about it and he was very remorseful and swore he would never do it again. So, as young and naive as I was, I believed him.

Meeting My Husband

And so, the wedding would go ahead as planned. Mum and Dad were paying for almost everything for the wedding as that was our culture. The bride's parents paid for the wedding – except for the alcohol and the hiring of the suits and cars which was paid for by the groom. So, we had to save some more money for that.

The wedding day came and it was a beautiful, sunny September day. It all went really well. We rented a granny flat which was very old but we were only paying AUD$18 a week in rent. Believe me, that's all it was worth. The people that owned the house had chickens and rabbits and it used to encourage rats to come in the yard. I'll leave that there.

Antonia and Philippa (Mum) at her first wedding.

Antonia's parents at a wedding.

I stared to get sick and had infection after infection – all while wondering why, as I kept a very clean house. Soon after, I found out why because I would open my drawers and find cockroaches there all the time. And I always used to hear noises in the roof of our granny flat.

One day, we were just lying in bed and there was a lot of noise in the roof and you wouldn't believe it. There was this rat's tail hanging from the man hole!

That did it for me; I was not staying there another night. I started raking my brain as to where we were going to live. My twin sister and her husband had bought a house and I asked them if we could live with them until we found somewhere else. They said it was okay to stay there for a little while. I went and told the landlord what was happening, and we were out of there that same weekend. We lived at that granny flat for a year.

While we were living at my sister's place, Vic got hold of the money we had, as by then we had a shared account. He started to gamble heavily and I was always crying into my pillow wondering where my life was going. I couldn't see us ever having our own home or having children. So I decided to take full control again and only have the bank account in my name. That way he couldn't touch it.

I knew we had to move from my twin sister's place at some point, and my youngest sister Rita and her husband bought a home that had a granny flat with it, which was separated from the house and was much bigger than the last granny flat we lived in and much cleaner.

It had one bedroom, small kitchen and combined dining room and a combined laundry and shower. So we asked if we could live there and pay them the rent. They were happy with that. I think we were paying them AUD$25 a week, which was still very cheap.

We were happy living there and got on with our lives and started to build up our bank account again. Because Vic was doing so well and not gambling, I decided to trust him again and teach him the value of saving. So, I put the account in both names, so he could feel a sense of achievement and know what it felt like to have money and be able to buy what you want or need. In a way, it was like having a small child and not a husband.

After a year living there, we had saved up enough money to buy a block of land to build our house. The land cost AUD$14,000, but it was not registered and we only had to put a small deposit down. It took over 12 months for the land to be registered, and by then, we were doing really well with our savings as Vic was behaving himself and not gambling. So, by the time the land was registered, we had the money to pay off the land, which again, was another great achievement.

Just two weeks before we were to pay the land off, Vic decided to gamble again and he lost a lot of money. Because he was too scared to tell me that he lost some money, he continued to gamble to try and get some back, as gamblers do, but he lost the lot. He still didn't know how to tell me and when I went to check exactly how much money we had in the account before we were to pay the land off, I again got a much bigger shock and I think my heart stopped for a while.

I was fuming with rage and right there and then, I thought my life was over. I would never be happy or have anything ever again in my life.

When Vic came home, he knew he was in big trouble and we had a big argument, but somehow we got through it again. I had to tell the company we bought the land from that we couldn't afford it and we lost the deposit. But imagine how hard this was to explain to my family that Vic lost all our money again. He felt uncomfortable with my family as he always felt guilty about what he did and felt he was being judged, which was understandable on both sides.

We went along with life again and this time, I put the account in my name, even though I knew starting from the beginning again was going to be tough. I left the company I was working for and got a job closer to home in a factory making jackets and trousers.

Meeting My Husband

The money was a little better and since I refused to be beaten, I started the daunting task of trying to save a deposit for a house. It was very slow going but we were doing okay again.

By this time, we were married for three years and I felt I hadn't achieved anything in my life yet and wanted to have a baby to fill the void.

Chapter 10

Starting a Family

I was so overjoyed when we found out I was pregnant that I called Mum straight away from a public phone and then called my twin sister Salvina. I couldn't wait until we started to buy some baby clothes – even though I made most of them as I was handy with sewing machine and it was a lot cheaper anyway. I borrowed the cradle and pram from my sister, so we basically had everything ready to go.

I had a trouble-free pregnancy and gave birth to our beautiful daughter, Lisa. Vic was beside himself; he was the happiest man alive. He went and got her a Valentine's card as three days after she was born, it was Valentine's Day. I still have that card today. I thought now that Vic has a baby to love and look after, he wouldn't gamble anymore. After all, he had responsibilities; a wife and child.

I was in hospital for six days, so he had to look after things at home. And of course, he got paid while I was in hospital and wasn't there to put the money in the bank. He got tempted and cleaned out our account. This time, he forged my signature; he was so desperate to win it back before I came out of hospital.

I could see there was something wrong when he came to pick me up from the hospital; the look of guilt on his face was enough. I didn't say anything as part of me was praying and hoping there was nothing wrong. After all, I had a beautiful baby girl to focus on and look after. I just didn't want to think about it. I just wanted to enjoy my new baby who I loved with all my being.

I was a natural mother and wasn't nervous at all with feeding, bathing or changing. I was only home for a few days from hospital, and since we lived near the shopping centre, I put Lisa in the pram and went to the bank to get some money out for shopping. I knew Vic cleaned out our account, but not to the point where we didn't have enough money to buy bread or milk. It was a good thing I was breastfeeding the baby. So, we made do with what food we had in the house and waited until the next payday to shop.

We had to have Lisa in our room as we were still living in a one-bedroom granny flat. I was getting pretty restless living there with a baby as there just wasn't enough room for all the other baby stuff that was needed.

Lisa was only three months old when I approached my old employer and asked if I could work from home sewing jackets and trousers. He agreed but I had to buy an industrial sewing machine. Not only

Starting a Family

did I not have enough room for Lisa's stuff, but I now had to make room for an industrial sewing machine. I put it in place of the pram and started working in between Lisa's sleeping and feeding times.

Sometimes, I would be up all hours of the night to make as much as I could as I used to get paid by how many pieces I made. I was determined to save as much as I could to try and get ourselves out of the granny flat.

It wasn't easy working from home as I was so housebound. I felt I had no interaction with the outside world. If I wasn't looking after Lisa, I was sewing. I gave it up after a year and decided to get a job at an RSL club waitressing. At least I was interacting with adults again. It worked out well as I was able to look after my own baby during the day and her father looked after her at night.

Vic started to work a lot of overtime and the money I was earning was okay. We had to prove that we could save money regularly if we wanted to apply for a loan. We started looking for houses to work out how much we needed and we found a brand new, three bedroom house with no garage that was near completion. We worked out that by the time it was completed we would have saved enough for the deposit. I was putting away every cent I could for that deposit. We managed to save the 20% that was needed.

Back then, there was a type of loan you could apply for if you were on a low income. We applied for it and were successful and was locked in at 5%. We bought the house when Lisa was eight months old, and moved into it when she was 11 months old.

Secrets of a Maltese Girl

We had no curtains or blinds for the windows, no carpet or tiles on the floor. The only furniture we had was a wardrobe, a bed for us and Lisa's borrowed cot and her little wardrobe. I put sheets on the windows and borrowed beanbags to sit on. We also had our dining room table and chairs from the granny flat.

The house felt so big compared to the granny flats we lived in for the past four years. I was so happy to finally move into my own home and have Lisa's first birthday in our own home. We had all her cousins from both sides at her party and she was devouring her first birthday cake in her pink and white frilly dress.

We really needed to put some floor coverings as it was getting cooler and as Lisa didn't learn to crawl on her hands and knees but waddled around on her bottom. She tore so many of her pants as the floors were bare timber. We couldn't afford the carpet, but we managed to get the window coverings first as they had three months interest free. I made sure I paid them off before the three months. Then, we got the carpet put in 12 months later, also on three months interest free.

It was slow going but we were getting there. We had no lawn in the backyard as we couldn't afford to buy it, so I used to get runners from neighbouring houses and plant it. By the time summer came, Lisa would be able to play in the backyard. It grew and grew, and by the end of summer, we had a lovely lawn.

I was content with life being a Mum during the day and working at one restaurant some nights, and club other nights. And Vic was a really good Dad; he would do anything that was needed for Lisa.

Starting a Family

He would play with her for hours and used to tape her singing nursery rhymes while he danced with her. He read to her and made up stories. She caught on about the stories when she got a little older; he could no longer pull the wool over her eyes.

He was still gambling, but I only allowed him so much money each week and monitored him so closely, as I didn't want to lose what we had. I could never really let my guard down with him. I was always on edge and couldn't relax worrying he would gamble more than he should. But all in all, life was going pretty well and I thought it was time for us to have another baby.

I was over the moon when in 1981, I gave birth to a son Stephen and didn't sleep for days with excitement knowing I had a pigeon pair. It made it a little easier to decide if I wanted more children or not. I felt that with the gambling problem Vic had, we couldn't afford more children as I wanted the very best for them – especially in the education department.

Stephen was the perfect baby and I was besotted with him; I would watch him sleep and then couldn't resist picking him up and holding him. He was an intelligent child and I'll never forget before he was even two, he could say hippopotamus so clearly. My children became the reason for my happiness and existence. I loved dressing them up and showing them off. Because we couldn't afford much, I would make their clothes and they were always well dressed. I always said that when I had the second baby, I would stay home for 12 months, but by the time Stephen was six months old, I had to go back to work as money was running low.

Secrets of a Maltese Girl

I got a job working a few nights at *Pizza Hut*. It worked out really well as I was still breastfeeding him. I would feed him before I left for my shift and again when I got home. I enjoyed working there as it fitted in well with the children. I had the best of both worlds as I was able to be home with them through the day and their father would look after them in the night when I was at work.

When Lisa was three, I sent her to preschool one day a week to prepare her for school later on and to give me some alone time with Stephen. She loved going and soon learnt how to write her name. She loved learning and would get so frustrated if she didn't get something right straight away. She always had to be the best in everything she did.

The time came when she had to go to school. I sent her to the local public school as we only had one car and couldn't get public transport to the nearest Catholic school. Being 'Miss Independent', Lisa loved school and settled in no time.

The school had a concert and she wanted to be in it. Since she was learning dancing, she decided to do her ballet dance. She had this beautiful tutu with a blue trim and she looked a picture. Well, she got up there and did a tremendous dance and came second in the concert. After that, there was no stopping her. She entered in anything and everything, and so she kept us very busy.

She excelled in most subjects but had a little problem in maths, just like me. Her year three teacher told me that she would always be average. I didn't like the word average, and since I couldn't help her with my bad maths record, I decided to get her a maths

Starting a Family

tutor. We couldn't really afford it, but we had to give her the best opportunity. She improved a great deal and went along in leaps and bounds.

I also put Stephen in preschool one day a week and he cried each time I took him. It broke my heart to leave him there, but I had to do it, as he needed to get used to it before he started school. Stephen was very attached to me and was always a very well behaved child, so I didn't have to yell at him much. He wasn't as strong headed as Lisa was.

I couldn't believe that when he started school, he would also cry for me every day I took him. When Lisa was in year five, and Stephen was in year two, I decided to send them to a Catholic school as I felt they needed to have a Catholic education. Even though I took them to church every Sunday, I couldn't teach them everything about our faith.

My sisters also had children of their own, so we spent a lot of time together. We would visit each other all the time. It was good for us and our children as they weren't just cousins; more like brothers and sisters. We would exchange clothes and toys all the time. We would take them out on picnics at the beach and go shopping together. You really don't need much money to do the simple things in life.

And when it came to holiday times – like Easter or Christmas – we would rent a house together at the Central Coast and our children would have a ball together. Those are the fondest memories of our children and I hold them close to my heart.

The children would always be writing plays and creating dances to perform for us. We all made sure to nurture our children's talents with every opportunity available. We all got them music lessons. Some learnt the piano, while others learnt guitar, trumpet and violin.

My children in particular were very keen in sport. Lisa loved running, so we got her involved in a running club and she was the youngest runner in the club to run a 3.5km run at five years old. Her father used to run marathons for the same club, so I suppose that encouraged her more. Stephen was soccer mad from the age of four, both indoor and outdoor, and was always great at it. He was also a very good tennis player but had a bit of a temper when he lost. He still plays soccer till this day. We also had them involved in little athletics. Lisa also had a love of dancing so she learnt tap, ballet and jazz and continued into her 20s. We were running around with them from one place to another for their sporting activities, but it was all worth it.

I wanted to get a new job that earned more money and could still work around the children's school hours. My sister Rita was doing door to door sales, selling *World Book Encyclopaedias*. Yes, encyclopaedias. She was earning really good money and was very good at it. I decided to attend a sales meeting and thought to myself, *"I can't do this. I can't go knocking on peoples doors."*

I was too proud and a bit shy, too. But my sister convinced me to try it. I did a sales training course with the company, bought my kit which was the minimum as I couldn't afford the whole kit and went out with my sister for a few times to observe. She averaged at least four sales out of six door knocks.

Starting a Family

It was time for me to go at it alone. I was so scared to go out and knock on doors on my own, but I had to do it sooner or later. I managed to get in a couple of doors and did my pitch, which was pretty raw, but it was practice for me. I went out again and did another pitch and didn't get the sale. I was feeling pretty down by then, so I asked my sister to come out with me again and she said, *"You have to do it alone if you want to learn."*

I was angry with her and said to myself, *"I can't do this."*

Well, the bomb fell again and my husband gambled all our savings, so I was desperate once again to earn money to get us out of the debt. He didn't want to tell me he lost money so he went and borrowed money on very high interest rate to pay off the gambling debt. I got extremely angry about the situation he put us in again.

I was determined not be beaten as there was no way my children were going to miss out and give up their music and dancing lessons because their father couldn't provide for them the way he should have.

I asked my manager if he could go out on the field with me to see how he did his pitch and sales. He made the sale and I said to myself, *"He is nowhere near as good as Rita. If he can get sales, then I should be able to."*

The next day, after I took the children to school, I chose an area and started knocking on doors. I got in a couple of doors and made my first sale. That was encouraging enough for me to want to go out again. The money I made for that sale was what I earned working three nights at a restaurant.

Secrets of a Maltese Girl

Every week, we would have meetings with our sales team, which was a positive thing as we would build each other up. When I saw people from my team making two to three sales a week, it encouraged me to do the same. I knew I could earn really good money here and it would get us out of some debt. Every spare moment I had, I would open up one of the books and learn more about what was in them, so I could do a better pitch next time.

I started to feel a little more confident now and went out on my own again while the children were at school. I went into an area where I knew there were young families and made a pitch and was successful in getting the sale. My sister Rita was my team leader and she had a manager above her. We discussed prospect of going out as teams, so we asked this lovely older man that was part of our team if he would like to come out on the field with us.

We would meet up in different areas and partner up with someone different each week. This worked out great as it was safer for all of us. This became a regular thing and we all looked forward to it as we would have a break and meet up for lunch at a nice cafe or Chinese restaurant – and so, it became a social thing also for me.

I started to feel really confident now and was making two to three sales a week. We would go to the office to take our orders in and have our weekly meetings. The company had incentives for us, and there were prices depending on the amount of sales we had, so it really made me want to go out there and sell as much as I could. Not only for the prizes but the good money I was earning.

Starting a Family

It was such great fun ordering prizes from the catalogue. Most of the time, I would choose gifts for the children and sometimes, I would choose something for me or the house. I felt we all needed a holiday, even though we had some debts we needed to clear. So I set a goal for myself and if I reached it. I was going to take all of us to Fiji.

I advised both my husband and the children that I would need their support if I was going to reach my goal. They had to be well behaved and do their homework and chores. I also said to them that if they did that, I would give them AUD$10 for every sale I made. I worked out I needed about AUD$4,000 to take the four of us to Fiji. And I had to be very strict that the money was put away only for our holiday and not the outstanding debts.

Well, the children made some serious money as I was selling around two to three sets a week, so they were making an average of AUD$30 a week each. This was a fair bit of money for such young children. It was a good incentive and became a combined effort. So, I reached my goal and off we went to Fiji and a great time was had by all of us.

Things got serious now and the company had a sales conference every year in America. We were given the opportunity to win the trip and included in this trip was a Canadian holiday. We had to sell an average of five full sets of encyclopaedias and other products with it.

We were given a few months to do this, so I started to get excited and plan how I was going to do this and win the trip. You see – it wasn't just the trip for myself, but the opportunity to get ourselves out of debt. I advised my family that I would be very busy in the next few months. I reminded them about how we worked together last time and how they got their reward at the end of it. Except this time, their reward would be the gifts I would get for them when I came back. My husband was okay with looking after the children while I was away. He was very capable of looking after them, but not so much with the money side. But I had to take a chance and do something for me this time.

I worked really hard and tried to stay as motivated as much as I could. When you are in sales, you could be on top of the world one day and down in the dumps the next. But I knew that and just went with my blinkers on. Nothing was going to get in my way.

My sister Rita and I did a lot of work together and had lots of laughs with some of the people we met along the way. We came across some of the most wonderful and interesting people and heard so many stories from them. Some about their struggles in coming to Australia, and how they got here. Others being forced to leave their country and how they escaped and some who had to leave their children and wives behind. It reminded me of how it was for us when we came to Australia. It was so humbling to see these parents wanting so much for their children.

Many times, they would want us to stay for dinner once the pitch was finished and signed up to buy them. When the books were delivered, I would go back and show the children how to use them, as the parents were concerned they couldn't help them. I understood how they felt as I was one of those children that didn't get any help. They would be so appreciative of the extra service I offered them. Not only did I make a good income from pitching and selling these books, but I also got so much satisfaction of seeing these children so excited about them. I was also educating myself about the many different nationalities and cultures I presented these books too, and their way of life.

I made many friends on this journey and know that some of these children grew up to do great things. You see, they saw the opportunities on offer when they came to Australia and grabbed it with both hands. They appreciated the opportunities Australia had to offer – as my family did when we came all those years ago.

I went out with full force and was selling an average of four to five sets of encyclopaedias a week. Every time I sold a set, I would call my sister Rita and share the excitement with her, and she would also tell me about her sales. We would so look forward to going to our weekly meetings to see who was on target for winning the trip.

We were both on target and of course, it just made me more determined and motivated as I was getting a lot of recognition from the company – not to mention all the prizes I was winning. I was like a little girl in a toy store, bringing so many useful gifts for both children and myself. Not only that the income I earned was able to pay off all our debts – except the house – but I was able to put some money back in the bank. It was an amazing feeling.

My sister and I were the highest achievers most weeks which also meant a promotion was coming in the near future. The end of the competition period was nearing and I was working long hours to try and reach my goal. I was short one sale and only had two days to do it.

I was not going to be beaten, so Rita came out with me on the field for support. We were going to get that sale, no matter what.

I finally got the sale the night before our weekly team meeting.

We got to our meeting early and there was a lot of anticipation from other members of our team wondering who reached their goal and who didn't. Out of the whole team, there was just a handful who won the trip, and it was announced that my sister's team had the highest sales score in the whole competition. You see, my sister introduced other people into the company and built herself a really good sales team.

There was a lot of excitement when it was announced that both my sister and I won the trip. I was only with the company a little less than a year when I won my first major trip. A few weeks after that, it was announced that my sister was promoted to manager of the team, and I was promoted to team leader. Rita was extremely good at her job and was also great at training people both in the office and out on the field. She was asked to do a talk at the conference in America in front of 4,000 people.

I don't know how I managed to do all this while I was trying to reach my goal, as my dad got really sick and was diagnosed with stomach cancer. They operated on him and said there was nothing they could do for him and he only had a very short time to live.

Back then, we didn't know the type of cancer it was, but later learnt it was mesothelioma. Mum advised us that she didn't want Dad to know the seriousness of his illness. And when I suggested that he should know, she wouldn't allow us to visit him on our own just in case we told him he had cancer and was dying.

Unfortunately, Dad suffered a stroke one week after his operation and lost his ability to talk. We were then allowed to see him and he would look straight into my eyes wanting to say something but nothing came out of his mouth. It was so sad to see him like that. Sadly, Dad died only four weeks from the time he was diagnosed. He was only 72 years old.

We had his funeral and it was a lovely celebration of his hard and very difficult life. We all grieved him in our own way.

Chapter 11

My Big Trip

The time came for me to fly out on my first combined conference and holiday. We flew to Chicago first for the conference and then San Francisco and Washington. When we got to Chicago, we had a day of guest speakers which was held at one of the big theatres. There were people from all over the world there representing their countries. One of the special guests was my sister Rita.

I was so proud of her and she did a tremendous job. If it wasn't for her introducing me to the company and encouraging me, I wouldn't been in the best financial position I was in at that time. I learned about so many aspects of life when meeting so many wonderful people at that conference, from the professionals to the ordinary everyday people. Because of her, I became stronger and wiser and more determined to succeed.

Don't get me wrong, I did the hard yard but someone had to start me off, and that was my dear sister Rita. It just so happened she also wrote a book about sales and how to start your own business and be successful.

The next day, there was a formal night and we were looking forward to it as this also meant presentation night for the high achievers. It was a great night and the food was to die for. I had never been to such an amazing night. After the meal, the formalities started and it was announced that my sister Rita got the top award for the highest personal sales and top team. She was presented with a beautiful trophy and they also announced she would be the director of the team.

Then, shortly after, my name was announced for top personal sales with a similar trophy and was promoted to manager of our team. It didn't get better than that; we were very proud of ourselves. Not a bad effort for two sisters from a poor background, right? I believe if you want something bad enough, you can achieve it. You just have to put in the hard work and have lots of determination.

After our conference in Chicago, it was time to have some fun, so we all headed to San Francisco and were all given white t-shirts with the company logo on it to wear on a cruise they had organised for us. If you didn't have that white t-shirt, you couldn't get on board.

While we were waiting to get on the boat, they had the full rock n' roll band and dancers, complete with old motor bikes and cars, for us on the dock. It was such a wonderful experience, we felt like royalty. From there, we went on to Washington DC and had a private tour of the *White House*.

My Big Trip

It was time for our Canadian part of the trip, and what a trip that was! We covered a lot of Canada, but the company didn't disappoint when we did the Rockies. They took us to Hells Gate and as we entered, they had a full Scottish band directing us over the Hells Gate Bridge. It was one of my favourite trips of all time. I had a great time but I missed my children very much. The trip came to an end and it was time to go home.

Rita and Antonia at Niagra Falls.

Chapter 12

More Unwelcome Surprises

When I got home, I was ever so glad to see my children and spoiled them with gifts. When I saw my husband, I could tell there was something wrong, as he wouldn't look at me. He had that guilty look on his face, and I could always tell when he got up to no good. I thought to myself, *"What surprises has he got for me now? Is there no rest for the wicked?"*

I just wanted to settle in with the children before I find out what he got up to. We didn't have internet banking back then to check our accounts or credit cards. You had to go to the bank and produce a savings book.

I waited for a few days and decided to go to the bank and yes, he did it again. I had to give him authority to use the account, as I was away for two and a half weeks and he needed to do shopping and pay the children's before and after school care fees. He had gambled all our money away again.

When I approached him, he blamed it on me this time because I went away and left him to look after things. He said he felt abandoned by me, poor man. I couldn't believe what he was saying.

All the times I had gotten us out of trouble and the sacrifices I made to make this marriage work and keep a roof over our heads. It was okay for me to work so hard and take the family for a holiday instead of him doing it, but as soon as I did something for myself, he fell to pieces, because I wasn't there to mother him.

I felt so deflated and alone again; I just didn't know how I was going to pick myself up. I had such a good time and was on a real high when I was promoted and won my award. I thought, *"How I am going to be able to concentrate and live up to my responsibilities with my team and employer? How was I going to do that when I was not motivated myself?"*

I knew that if I was to get through this feeling, I had to go out on the field straight away, as the longer I waited, the harder it was going to be.

I had a lot of thinking to do regarding Vic's actions and I kept thinking I can't continue to keep getting him out of trouble all the time – he needs to take responsibility.

More Unwelcome Surprises

A week after I got back from my trip, I dropped the children at school and went out to try and do some pitching, but it was very difficult as I felt I was being forced to go out and continue to be the provider. I couldn't close a sale for a week as I wasn't fully focused with worrying about how we were going to catch up again with our finances.

I was getting very frustrated and angry about the whole situation. Eventually, I did start to get sales again and was earning good money. But I was still angry with Vic as I had the entire financial burden on my shoulder and felt it was very unfair to the children with me feeling this way as they could pick up on the tension in the house between us.

I said to him, *"You need to get some help as I won't put up with it if you continue to keep putting us in debt."*

He agreed to see a councillor, so I found one for him and he was seeing her every week.

The councillor gave him some exercises to do at home, like going into a room on his own for an hour every day to meditate. He did this as soon as he came home from work, which meant I had to keep the children quiet or I would have to take them to their activities after school. I was patient as I was thinking that it would be worth it at the end.

He was also told he couldn't listen to the radio so he wouldn't be tempted, and if his work colleague talked about gambling, he had to just walk away. He was doing all this for quite a while and he seemed to be doing okay.

Secrets of a Maltese Girl

Believe it or not, he actually went without gambling for three months and I thought we were getting somewhere.

Just when I thought things were going pretty well, and he was giving me his pay packet every week, he got tempted again and blamed it on his friends, because they would be talking about gambling and he couldn't help it. He got to the point where he was taking the children's money from their money boxes, which was obviously desperation. And I had noticed that things started to go missing from the house.

I knew things were getting pretty bad and I had to do something. I couldn't talk to Mum about it as she had dealt with way too many problems of her own to have to deal with mine. So mostly, I talked to my twin sister Salvina and Rita about it. I told them of my intention to leave him as he can't keep depending on me to get him out of trouble all the time; he needed to stand on his own two feet and take responsibility.

I knew he couldn't afford to move anywhere else, so it was decided that the children and I move into Rita's house for a while until we found him somewhere to live. I approached Vic and told him I had had enough. I said to him, *"I can't do this anymore as I'm always on edge, and it isn't fair on Lisa and Stephen to see what's going on."*

He started to get very agitated and said, *"I'm not going to move from our house as I can't afford it."*

I told him of my intentions to stay with my sister while I tried to find a place for him to live in. He was hesitant but accepted it in the end.

More Unwelcome Surprises

We moved into one room at my sister's place which was extremely difficult and only took the bare necessities like the children's clothes and school stuff and just a few clothes for me. We cooked together and shared the house chores. I had to drive them to school every day as my sister lived a little far from the school they attended.

I knew I couldn't do this for long as I missed my house and so did the children and thought it was not fair for us to be away from our house.

We didn't create the problem, he did.

The children started to argue with their cousins and it started to create some friction in my sister's house, so after six weeks, I moved us back home and tried to give it another go. Vic still couldn't afford to move out, so I had no choice in the matter. I was doing all this and trying to work at the same time, which was very difficult, but I had to have some income.

We went along with our lives as best as we could and I told Vic he had to try again to beat this habit. This time, we went to our family doctor and told him his problem and he referred him to a psychiatrist. He also gave him some things to work on at home. Vic was trying very hard and went to see a hypnotist to try and beat it.

With me leaving him for those few weeks frightened him, so he was trying really hard as he knew he had nowhere to go. His family weren't very supportive. I suppose they had seen it enough times and had their own families to worry about.

He was doing pretty well and we were getting back on track again. I was doing well with my work. I had put some savings away for the many rainy days we always seemed to have. The children were getting older and they were having friends over all the time. We had a three bedroom house and one lounge. Computers were being introduced and I felt we needed a study, play room and another bathroom.

So we talked about it and started drawing some plans. We were getting very excited at the prospect of extending our home. It finally felt good to be doing something major and know we could afford it. We called a couple of builders to give us a quote, and we decided on this particular builder as he was very well known in the area.

Even though we had some savings, I wanted to save more so we wouldn't have such a big loan to pay off, along with our housing loan. I was always thinking ahead as I never knew what to expect with Vic's gambling problem.

Interest rates started to go up and they went as high as 17% that year. So I really had to make sure we had most of the money to pay for it, as our loan would be way too high for us to manage. It was all going really well and it looked great.

I went to the bank to organise the payment and found out that again, Vic got tempted and withdrew all the money.

My heart just stopped with the shock and I was so close to collapsing. I couldn't believe he did this to us again.

More Unwelcome Surprises

Nothing I did to help him seemed to have made any difference. So I was trapped in this financial rollercoaster again. I took it up with him but it didn't get me anywhere. So, we had to borrow the whole amount and pay it off on the 17% interest.

Chapter 13

Doris' Health Struggles

My sister Doris had difficulties falling pregnant and tried IVF three times which all failed. After eight years or so, they decided to adopt, however, because they were older, they couldn't adopt a new baby. They could only adopt a baby that was 18 months old or more. So, they looked at adopting one from Korea as the waitlist in Australia was about eight to 10 years.

They got the ball rolling and were told it would take about two years or so. So they decided to go on a long awaited holiday; a cruise. A great time was had by both obviously, as when they got back a few weeks later, they announced they were pregnant. What joy after 10 years of trying?

Secrets of a Maltese Girl

The pregnancy was going along well and Doris was nearing the end of it. On one particular Tuesday – when we would meet up at Mum's house for our regular visit – for some strange reason, I woke up feeling very uneasy and nervous that day and didn't know why.

By then both children had started school, so I dropped them off at school and continued on to Mum's house. Doris was just over eight months pregnant and she told us, *"I haven't felt the baby kicking for the last two days and have a very bad taste in my mouth."*

We urged her to go to the doctors and she made an appointment straight away. She went to see him that afternoon and she was told her baby had died. He advised her to wait until she went into labour and sent her home. It was the most devastating and saddest news I ever heard and couldn't believe it had happened to them – especially after trying for so long.

She went into labour two days later and gave birth to a stillborn son who they named Daniel. He was a big baby and died from the cord wrapped around his neck. They were both so devastated and Doris seemed to have aged so quickly and lost a lot of weight. The funeral was so very sad and my heart just broke for both of them.

While she was pregnant with Daniel, she didn't advise the adoption agency that she was having a baby. So, 18 months after she lost Daniel, they got a call to say they had a baby girl in Korea ready for them to adopt. They were over the moon as the dream of becoming parents was becoming a reality. The baby was 23 months old and was in foster care. In order to bond with the baby, they had to stay

Doris, Health Struggles

in Korea for two weeks. When they came back to Australia and Doris introduced her to the family, she fitted in really well.

Apparently, the adoption does not become legal until after two years as the real mother could change her mind and want the baby back. They couldn't wait for the two years to be over. So they got on with life with their new daughter, had their challenges with bringing up a child and Doris enjoyed being a mother finally.

After around six months or so, Doris started to lose a lot of weight and was having night sweats and not feeling well at all. She was going from one doctor to another to find out why this was happening. Test after test, they couldn't find an answer.

It was recommended that she go to a specialist, who then ordered an MRI and other blood tests. I went with her for support when the results came in. You could tell the news was not good. She was told that she was in the fourth stage of cancer which was called Non-Hodgkin's Disease. He advised her that she didn't have long to live, four to six weeks max. She was admitted to hospital that night to start treatment in the next few days. Poor women. As if she didn't have a bad enough life as it was.

The first thing she worried about was if the adoption agency finding out about her being sick they would take their daughter away from them. We assured her we would be there for her and help with their daughter wherever we could.

Her treatment consisted of chemotherapy every three weeks for six months. After that, they would do more scans to see if the treatment worked. She was very sick for a week after chemo and then she would pick up a little. So the days when she was on treatment and not well, we took turns to help out with her daughter and cooking for her husband.

The times where she was feeling a little better, she looked after their daughter on her own. After a couple of months into her therapy, her husband couldn't take the stress of it all and left his job. We thought this would make it easier, and it did a little. At least he was home and Doris could show him what needed to be done. Doris spoilt her husband and took control of everything. The finances, house chores and any decisions about their daughter. This was to her detriment as when it came time for him to look after things, he couldn't cope.

So, my sisters and I were always there when we were needed. There were times when she couldn't have her chemotherapy as her blood count was too low. So instead of being six months for her treatment, it ended up being eight months.

She finished her treatment, and scans were done to see if she beat her cancer. Good news, there didn't seem to be any sign of it so Doris was in remission. It was great to hear.

The doctors told her that if she didn't get it back within 10 years, she would probably never get it again. So she would have tests every three months to keep an eye on it. And a year or so later, she also got the good news that the adoption of their daughter was final. She was in no danger of losing her any longer.

Doris, Health Struggles

Life went on for Doris and her small family; her husband found another job with the help of my younger brother Nick. Unfortunately, 18 months after her last treatment, the cancer came back again.

This time they tried a different type of chemotherapy, and she was a very sick women. She started to lose faith and was very afraid that she wouldn't make it and watch her daughter grow up.

She fought really hard and I believe she had the strength only because of her daughter. She finished her treatment for the second time and was again, in remission.

It was good news but when you escape death twice, there will always be a shadow looming, as you always think it's going to come back.

Doris on her 40th birthday and during her second bout of cancer.

Chapter 14

Leaving My Husband

I continued to work hard in my sales work and knew I had to end this marriage in the near future as I could not do it anymore. It wasn't fair on the children to see me unhappy all the time. I wanted to enjoy my life and not have to constantly monitor Vic. I felt I had three children not two, and he was the hardest of them all.

I started to plan how I was going to leave, and when. So, I continued to work hard and long hours and was earning fairly good money. As I said before, the more he gambled the madder I got, the harder I worked. After three years, we managed to pay all the debt on the extension. We still had a mortgage but the payments were manageable.

I knew if I was going to do this, I couldn't have too much debt. I decided to buy a new car, so that once I was on my own, the car would last me for at least 10 years. I owned that car within the first 12 months. Then I started to put some savings away without Vic knowing as I knew when the time came to separate, he could not afford to pay me any child support for the children.

They were still costing a lot of money to educate and all the activities they had. Lisa had a horse and was learning piano and dancing. And Stephen was learning the guitar, soccer and tennis. And I didn't want them to have to give anything up because of their father's habit. This was going to be difficult enough for them.

Vic continued on and off gambling and I lost all, if any, respect I had for him, and we were growing apart more and more each day. There was a terrible altercation with him, and I knew I just didn't want to be in the marriage any longer, I had had enough and wanted out.

I engaged a lawyer and told her what has been happening. The conclusion was that we should go 65% for me and 35% for him. And he would have to pay child support for the children. In the meantime, I went to the bank and advised them of the situation and asked if I could get a loan to pay his share to him. They were able to offer me the loan after I showed them my earnings.

I approached him and told him I wanted to separate as I was tired of constantly putting up with his gambling. He wasn't shocked with what I had said. We both agreed that we had to talk to the children about our intentions. I felt relief that he didn't fight it, but at the same time I felt very sad that it has come to this – even though I knew it had to happen one day.

Leaving My Husband

I told him I had already seen a lawyer and how she thought the assets should be divided. I also said we have to come to a mutual agreement as I didn't want to argue and waste our money paying lawyers. No offence to any lawyers out there.

We knew we had to get one involved just to do the formalities. So I proposed to him that since the children still needed a few more years of Catholic education, I would need to have 65% and he would have 35% and said he would have to pay child support.

He didn't agree to it, so knowing that he probably wouldn't be able to pay child support anyway because of his habit, I proposed to him to leave the 65% to me and 35% to him and he wouldn't have to pay child support, and he agreed to it.

I told him I wanted to stay in the house as I didn't want to uproot the children and I would buy him out. He had no qualms about me buying him out as he could see the dollars signs and a way of paying his debts. We discussed it with the children and there were a lot of tears and sadness, and it broke my heart to see them go through that. But it had to be done.

Lisa was 15 years old at the time and Stephen was 12. It wasn't the best of timing as they were both teenagers. But it was never the right time. I just knew it had to be done if we were going to move forward.

We were legally separated, but Vic could not afford to move out until the money came through. So we lived under the same roof in different rooms for three months. This was the most difficult awkward situation to be in for both the children and me. In the meantime, I was constantly looking for somewhere for Vic to move into when the money came through. I didn't want him to live too far as he needed to see the children regularly.

There was no restrictions on how often he could visit the children. It was decided he could come and see the children anytime he wanted. As a matter of fact, he still came to dinner at least three times a week. And he picked up the children to take them to their activities many times. He was very good that way. I finally found him a granny flat at Kemps Creek which was only 20 minutes' drive from our place.

The day he moved out was a very sad day for myself and the children. I felt like someone just cut one of my arms off. After all, I knew him for 21 years. We shared two beautiful children and we also had some good times, mainly watching the children grow and succeed.

He wasn't a bad person; he just had a terrible habit and was always drowning us in debt. He had his reasons and I tried with all my being to help him but couldn't reach him in the end. It was really sad that only a couple of months after he moved out, the money from his part share of the house was already lost. I had a feeling that would happen. I pleaded with him to look after the money as I will not be there anymore to pick up the pieces.

I was so mad he did that as I was struggling to pay the mortgage and put the children through school, and he just blew it in a couple of months. He could have given some of it to the children. But instead, I later found out that when the children had casual work, he would go to them and ask for money. If I had known that then, I would not have been as nice to him. He put the children in very awkward situations.

It wasn't until many years later the children told me many stories about their fathers gambling habits. I thought I knew it all but they were protecting their father – which is natural, of course. After all, he was still their father and they loved him in their own way.

I thought the children were doing well considering the circumstances, but I was wrong. I was mainly worried about Stephen as he was the youngest. Lisa always had a strong character and thought she was handling things okay, but she wasn't.

I got a call from the year coordinator to set up a meeting and discuss Lisa's behaviour which was unusual. When we got home after talking to her year coordinator, poor Lisa poured her heart out on how she felt about our separation. She just cried and cried, which just broke my heart.

Stephen was a very angry young man also, after all, boys are supposed to look up to their fathers. I was so angry at their father for putting all of us through that. So it was decided that both Lisa and Stephen attend counselling to help them through this difficult time. The separation affected both of them more than I thought, even though they saw what was happening in our home.

I would get so mad at their father sometimes as he just lived in his own little bubble with not a care in the world and the responsibility of putting food on the table, paying a mortgage, school fees and whatever else was needed to run a household. He was oblivious to the many challenges teenagers have to go through. I had to navigate the best way I could to help them with these challenges on my own. But I guess he didn't have the means to deal with it, as he also had to navigate life on his own when he was young.

Even though I came from a large family, there was no support system from anyone except my twin sister Salvina and Rita. Life got busy and everyone had their own families to tend too. I plodded along and juggled work around the children as best as I could. No matter what, I made sure I was always home for them before and after school.

Chapter 15

Reinventing Myself

Now that we were living on our own, I had to look for alternatives in the job area, as I didn't want to leave the children alone at night while I worked.

My sister Rita decided to start her own party planning business selling shoes and handbags. She asked me if I wanted to work for her in my own hours. I said I would give it a go as I could do it mostly on weekends, and I wouldn't be away from the children at night.

I had to learn all about the different leathers, soles and heels. I approached family members and friends to set up some parties to present the shoes and bags. While I was doing that, I also decided to study and brush up on my office skills. I did that while the children were at school and managed to do some parties in people's homes, selling shoes and bags on the weekends while their father looked after them. Because I was studying for six months, I was able to receive some benefits from the government, which helped to supplement my income.

Just before I finished my course, I started applying for jobs in school hours and was successful. I worked in that job for a little over 12 months. It wasn't very secure employment so I decided to look for a local government job. I managed to get a job working for our local council during school hours, which was great.

I spent three years in childcare managing the office at one of the many centres the council owned. Then I moved to the building and planning section, which I enjoyed as I loved learning about the growth in the local area and looking at the many building applications that came in.

After nearly four years of being on my own, I decided that I needed to do something for myself as my life consisted of looking after the children, work, cooking and cleaning. The only outlet I had was visiting my sisters, and I certainly didn't have the money to go out.

I was reading through the local paper which I always enjoyed and came across an advertisement for the 40+ club. It was a new club formed by a Maltese woman and was designed for people over 40 to meet up go on outings such as walking, dining, bowling and shows. I thought it was a good idea and a fresh start for me. So I plucked up the courage to go to the first meeting.

There were six people there besides the organiser: two couples, myself and two other women. We introduced ourselves and got to know each other a little. We organised a weekend to go walking at the end of the month. The next Monday, another two people joined up. And the third week one more person turned up and his name was Gary.

It was agreed by all that a list of names and phone numbers be given to each one of us. This was so that if an outing was organised and someone didn't have any means of transport or couldn't make it at the last minute we would be able to notify someone in the group.

The first meeting Gary turned up; we happened to leave the premises at the same time. It was July and very cold. He asked me, *"Where is your car?"*

I replied, *"Right outside the door."*

As soon as he saw the car he said, *"I think you need new tyres."*

I should have known then that he was a car enthusiast as he couldn't stop talking about the car he had just bought. You might think I was bored with the car talk, but with eight brothers, there was always car talk, so I didn't mind.

We talked a little longer and asked each other where we lived and how many children each of us had. It was getting very cold outside and I had to be a little rude and say I needed to go home as my children were on their own. They were 16 and 18 at the time. I thought he was a nice enough guy who was old school, and I also thought he was Italian, but he was a fair dinkum Australian.

Secrets of a Maltese Girl

The next Monday, the phone rang and Stephen answered it. He said it was Gary and was taken by surprise and wondered what he wanted. I had only met him the week before. He called to ask if I needed a lift to the meeting. I told him it was out his way and that I'll see him there. He insisted it was fine and he would pick me up.

So I gave him my address and sure enough, he was right on time. I thought I would be uncomfortable being with him in the car as I have never gotten in a car with anyone else since my separation, but I was okay.

We just talked about things in general on the way, things like where we both worked and stuff. We got to the venue where we met each week and discussed where we would go for our next outing. The meetings usually took about one hour or so and it was time to leave. As we were leaving, he asked me if I wanted to stop for coffee on the way home and I agreed.

The only place that was open was McDonalds, so he parked the car outside and we started talking in the car. By the time we realised how late it was getting, I said, *"We should go in and have that coffee."*

By then, *McDonalds* had closed as they didn't have a 24-hour trading back then. So, we didn't get to have that coffee.

We both had a lot in common, hence we talked until nearly midnight. He took me home and I have to say, I thought about him most of the next day. He seemed very genuine.

Reinventing Myself

He called again and asked if he could pick me up again, and I agreed. I had a feeling he had other intentions – good ones though, of course.

From then on, he picked me up every week. About the forth week in, he asked me out. He said we would be going out with friends of his who he'd known for over 25 years. He thought it would be more comfortable for me if there was another couple joining us. I thought that was very thoughtful; he was such a gentlemen.

He picked me up from home and I introduced him to my children and they seemed to like him straight away. We went off to a club with an upmarket restaurant and I met his friends who I got along with instantly. We had an amazing time.

The restaurant we went to had a rose on the table for each of the ladies. Unfortunately, I forgot mine there, so when he asked me out again the next week, he had a big, beautiful bunch of flowers for me to make up for the one I left at the restaurant. How thoughtful was that?

I hadn't gotten flowers from anyone in years, so it was really nice to get them. I told my sisters Salvina and Rita that I had met someone and my sister Salvina said to be careful. I assured her he was a very nice man and was very comfortable being with him.

He called me every day and before we knew it, we were dating. I couldn't believe it as I hadn't dated in a very long time. It was a very nice feeling, but scary at the same time.

Secrets of a Maltese Girl

I would have him over for dinner a few times a week and other times, we went out as by then, the kids were old enough to be left alone for a little while. It was hard to balance life with Gary and look after the children's needs, but it was worth the effort I put into the relationship.

I felt a little guilty at the time as my ex-husband was going through a very difficult time financially again. He was in so much debt that he had to move out of the granny flat. I found him a caravan park to live in which was cheaper than the granny flat. The children were so embarrassed about it, and the sad thing was, they couldn't stay over at his place as he had no room for them.

It was difficult for me to tell him I had met someone, but I had to let him know. He was very upset as he actually thought one day we would get together again because he used to come for dinner a couple of times a week. No chance of that on my part. After I told him I had met someone, he wouldn't come for dinner, and only came to see the children when I wasn't home. Or he would see the children at soccer or netball or whatever activities they were doing at the time. It took him a long time to except I was with someone else.

Gary and I continued to go to the 40+ Club and to most of the outings as time allowed. So we saw each other nearly every day. He was very helpful in my house; he would do the lawns and home maintenance for me. He was very handy and just so happened to be a builder by trade.

It was time for me to meet his family and I was very nervous about it. I met his mum and she was such a lovely soul and very kind. I got on with her very well.

Reinventing Myself

Then it was time to meet his children. Gary had his youngest son and girlfriend living with him at the time and his other son and daughter lived with their mum. They came to his home for dinner once a week; I went over on one of those nights to meet them. They were a bit reserved and I felt some tension there. You could see Gary was embarrassed and I felt so sorry for him. I didn't mention anything to him about it as he felt bad enough. After dinner, we cleaned up, I said goodnight to everyone and went home.

Our relationship was going at a fast pace and by three months, we both knew it was serious. It was so good to be with someone that didn't swear every time he watched a game of football or lose his temper at a drop of a hat. Vic swore so much when he was listening to a horse race or watching football. I hated those days as the children were picking up on the swear words.

Gary and I started discussing our future together and six months into our relationship, we got engaged. I told my children first and they were so happy for us. And then told my sisters and they also were over the moon for us both as they really liked Gary and got on with him well.

Gary had a house of his own which was still mortgaged and I had my home also mortgaged. We decided that we wouldn't live in any of our homes as we wanted a fresh start in our own home. We decided to sell Gary's house first to buy a block of land and build our home. Gary would move into my home until the house was built and then sell mine so we could be mortgage-free. In the meantime, we also had to organise our wedding and honeymoon.

The prospect of building a home together was very exciting, so we started looking for that special home. We chose the house we wanted to build and made a few changes to it. It was a beautiful and comfortable home for Gary, myself and my two children.

The wedding was set for the 1st of November and everything was organised. My two children were to give me away. We also wanted his children to have some part in the wedding, but unfortunately they were not keen on that – which was disappointing for Gary.

All the invitations went out and everyone that was invited to the wedding came, and not one person declined. Gary was very respected and liked among his work colleagues and friends. The ceremony was very meaningful and lovely. We had our reception and my younger sister Rita said a lovely speech and Gary also did a wonderful one.

It was time to leave the reception and when we were saying our goodbyes, a close family member on Gary's side said to us, *"I hope this one will last"* – meaning the first marriage didn't. I was very offended by what she said and why she had to say it. I'm happy to say that we have now been married for 27 years, so yes, this one lasted.

Reinventing Myself

Gary and I at our wedding

So off we went to Vegas, *Disneyland* and Hawaii for our honeymoon. Gary had never gone overseas before and couldn't stop talking about it. We had such a great time. By the time we got back, our house was nearly complete. We moved in just four days before Christmas.

We settled into our married life and busied ourselves in the house. We enjoyed doing everything together. I loved being outside and I couldn't wait to finish the house work, so I could go outside and help Gary with the lawns and the gardens. Gary also helped with the house chores; he could do anything. The only thing Gary didn't do is cook. Can't have it all, I guess.

It was nice having a new home and having the room to entertain family and friends. We had Gary's family over for dinner every week. We also had many parties and celebrations at our house. Like Salvina's and Doris' surprise 25th wedding anniversary and Doris's 40th birthday party.

My youngest sister Rita always said when her 25th anniversary, came up she would like to renew her wedding vows. So I spoke to my other sisters about organising a celebrant to surprise her. We managed to get hold of all the people that were in their wedding party.

We had a lovely backyard and even had a wedding arch that had the loveliest white flowers around it. We decided to have a yellow and white theme, and it looked really lovely. So, I told my sister Rita and her husband that we were doing a family Sunday lunch at our place if they would like to come. The girls and I had many Sunday lunches together so they weren't suspicious.

Everyone came and cars were parked in other streets, so they wouldn't get suspicious. When they arrived and saw what we had done, they were in shock but loved it. A lot of good family times were had in our new home and we have a lot of good memories.

We were both still working and I said to Gary that I would like to work part-time, possibly three days a week as I wanted to enjoy our home and be able to have the time to cook good meals and keep a clean house and hopefully, be more relaxed. He was all for it and he said I didn't have to work if I didn't want to – but I had been working all my life and couldn't imagine not working or having to depend on him financially.

Reinventing Myself

One of my work colleague was due to have a baby and I knew she wanted to come back part-time after her maternity leave. So I approached her and asked if she would like to job share. She said she would and wanted to do two days. I spoke to my manager about the concept of job sharing. This had never been done in our department, so they had to take it to HR to discuss. It was decided that we would trial it for six months to see if it would work out. As much as I didn't like sharing a desk, I did everything in my power to make it work. In the end, it was approved as a permanent part-time position.

Gary and I were mortgage-free and we had some money left from the sale of my home. I came up with the idea of buying an investment property. I broached the idea to Gary and he wasn't very keen at the time and was a little scared. I assured him we could do it and it would be very good for us when it came time to retire. So, he relented and we both started to look for a property to buy. We found a new house that had just been completed, which became our first investment property.

Things was working well for us and three years later, we decided to buy our second investment property. This time, it was an older style home and we had to do a fair bit of work to it. But both Gary and I were not scared of hard work. So, we fixed it up and rented it out. It felt so good to be able to do this as I always knew if you managed your money well and worked together, you can achieve great things. Gary was still able to buy his many new cars and boats, as they were his passion, and we were able to have a comfortable life and went on wonderful holidays and often out to dinners and shows. I started to get a real interest in investing in homes. I was always checking out the best areas to buy and we managed to invest some more.

Doris started to feel unwell again and we feared the worst that her cancer was coming back. She started the rollercoaster of many tests, and sure enough, it came back – with a vengeance this time. She was in remission for nearly 10 years. The doctors said the chemotherapy was not going to help this time. It was suggested she should have a bone marrow transplant.

They wanted to test the siblings to see if any of us were compatible. But before they could test us, she became very ill and weak and ended up with pneumonia. We thought we were going to lose her then.

After a couple of weeks, she got a little stronger. Her specialist advised us the only thing that would save her life is to have a stem cell transplant. It was risky and not too many survive the procedure. So, they waited until she was strong enough to be given a big dose of chemotherapy. They did that and she was put in isolation so she wouldn't pick up any germs or viruses. And three weeks later, she had the stem cell transplant.

It was touch and go for a while and out of three people that had the transplant, only Doris survived. What an amazing fighter she was. Her specialist told her that the cancer shouldn't return because of the procedure she had.

Chapter 16

My Children

My son Stephen didn't want to go to Year 12, so I said to him that if he got some sort of apprenticeship, he could leave. He decided he wanted to become an electrician, so he got himself an electrical apprenticeship. He didn't have a licence as he was too young, so I had to take him to the station to catch the train. I was worried about him as he was so young, only 16 at the time. But I got used to it after a while.

Stephen at his Graduation.

He was doing really well and enjoyed it. He saved most of his money as his goal was to buy his first car. Within nine months, he had saved all the money to buy a car outright. There was no borrowing money to buy a car in this household. If you didn't have the money, you didn't buy it. He finished his apprenticeship and stayed at that job for a few years, until someone associated with the company offered him a sales position of electrical goods. He decided to give it a go and was doing really well. He was very well organised which surprised me, as he wasn't like that at home.

He was earning a good wage, so I encouraged him to buy an investment property for his future, and to give him a sense of accomplishment. So, we started looking but he couldn't really afford to buy close to where we lived, so we looked at the Central Coast as they were cheaper there. We found a little, old, two-bedroom house that needed a lot

My Children

of work. It was in a good position and had a good block of land. It needed a new kitchen, bathroom, floors and other odd jobs.

He bought it and Gary said he would help him do it up. The task of renovating his house begun, my brother Nick and his son also helped, and of course I did my bit, and it was great to see Stephen work on his first investment property. We all worked very hard to finish the house so he could rent it out and the transformation was amazing. Everyone did a great job.

I never discouraged my children from trying new things, but I knew that Stephen's job was very stressful as there were always targets that had to be met. He was getting really stressed and he knew he had to do something about it, so he decided to look for another job. He was interested in this particular one but didn't get an interview – although he kept persisting and calling them all the time. It wasn't the type of work he was used to but wanted the challenge anyway.

After a couple of months, they figured this guy is not giving up, so they asked him to come in for an interview. He went in and felt confident that he could do the job. A week later, they called him and advised him that he was successful in getting the position.

I was so happy for him at the success of getting this new job. In two years, he became a team leader and a couple of years after, he became the manager of the team. As a mother, I'm so very proud of him and his accomplishments.

Stephen also became interested at investing in many properties. He is now the general manager of sales and travels all over the world for his job and manages to organise his travels around his beloved soccer.

My daughter Lisa finished her higher school certificate and considering her entire life had revolved around sport, it made sense that she wanted to go to university to study Sports Science. She got the marks she needed to get into the University of her choice and enrolled in a Bachelor of Human Movement studies specialising in Sports Science.

She worked hard during her degree and held down two jobs in personal training to get her through.

She excelled in her studies and was always in the top of her year. She was invited to do her honours year at the completion of her degree and received a scholarship to fund her studies. She graduated at the age of 22 with First Class Honours, 1A – the highest grading you can receive.

It was no surprise that she was then offered a scholarship from the University of Sydney to do her PhD. She accepted with open arms. She was still living with us and knew she would have our full support.

She chose to focus on the biomechanics of elite track and field athletics, which was her passion since she was a young child. She specialised in the long jump take off technique and worked with the *Sydney 2000 Olympic* track and field team, travelling all over Australia to collect her important data. One of her athletes even received a silver medal!

My Children

Lisa at her Graduation.

However, it was a hard slog. She was isolated and put in a significant amount of self-driven hours. I brought her many a cup of tea and sandwich while she was powering her way through research.

Lisa also worked as a tutor and lecturer at multiple universities during this time. With her scholarship, the income from her employment and being able to save aggressively while living at home, saved a fair bit of money and decided to buy a property not far from the city. I thought that was a bit ambitious of her.

Nonetheless, knowing her determination has no end, we started the search and there was some real rubbish out there. But we didn't give up and found one that was just getting fully renovated in a very expensive area in the Inner West of Sydney.

We negotiated the price and she was successful in buying the townhouse. She took a big chance on this, as she was still working on her PhD. Looking back, this is where her passion of property began.

Lisa's had a best friend who lived next door; they knew each other from the time they were four month's old. They did lots of things together and had many sleepovers. They danced in the same dance school, performed in competitions together. They both had a horse and rode together. It was a beautiful friendship.

Once Lisa started university and had a boyfriend, she didn't see a lot of her friend anymore. Time passed, and they started spending time together again, and it was like they never had a break at all. They decided to go on a road trip on the Easter weekend. Her friend loved driving and I was so worried about the two of them going on

My Children

such a long trip on their own. A good time was had by both of them and thank God, they got home safely.

Six weeks after their little adventure, they organised to meet up at a place close to where she lived. When Lisa got there, her friend hadn't arrived, but it wasn't unusual for her friend to be late. After an hour or so, Lisa started to worry and called her friend's sister to ask if she knew where she was. She told her she had spoken to her in the afternoon but had to cut the call short as she was going out herself. Lisa also called me to say her friend hadn't turned up.

I said, *"Maybe she had forgotten she was to meet up with you as it's a long weekend so maybe she went away somewhere."*

Lisa and her friend's sister searched around the area to see if they could see her car anywhere but to no avail. I called Lisa a couple of times on her mobile to see if she turned up, but she hadn't.

Lisa came home very early the next morning, and of course, extremely worried that something had happened to her friend. Gary and I went to visit his mum the next day and my mind was on Lisa's friend, and I just had this horrible feeling that something was terribly wrong. I tried to get it out of my mind and convinced myself that she just forgot she was meeting up with Lisa.

But when we were on our way home from visiting, I got a call on my mobile from Lisa hysterical, screaming, crying, and breathless and my blood went cold. I also went numb as I knew something terrible had happened. I asked Lisa if she was driving and she said she was.

I pleaded with her to stop the car as I was afraid she would have an accident. She was in such a state, but I managed to settle her down a little and she stopped the car by the side of the road. She told me that her friend had died. I went numb but had to try and stay calm for Lisa as she still had to drive home.

We got home and Lisa told me what had happened to her friend. She had been murdered and security found her body in bushland. She was killed the night she was supposed to meet up with Lisa. We were devastated and all I could think about was how the hell her parents and sibling were going to get over this.

Her mother and I had a many discussions about our children and both said that if anything ever happened to our children, we wouldn't want to live. They were the first words I thought about when I found out she had died. That weekend changed Lisa's our lives forever. Until this day, they haven't found the person who did it.

She was grieving for her friend so much and was a closed book about it. Every time I asked her anything, she wouldn't talk about it, and withdrew when it came to the subject. She would say they were her private thoughts when it came to her best friend and didn't want to share them with anyone.

I thought it was strange that she was going out a lot while she was grieving for her; I didn't understand it. I wanted to learn more about how people grieved in different ways. So I went to the library and borrowed a book to learn how I could help Lisa. After reading this book, I understood her way of grieving. I'm extremely thankful that she didn't get into drugs or alcohol to deal with her grief.

My Children

Before all this had happened, Gary and I expressed the idea that we wanted to start doing some travelling. So we started doing little trips in Australia for a couple weeks at a time as we were still working. And then we booked a trip to Hong Kong which was so different.

I wanted Gary to see the country where I was born, so we booked a one-month holiday, with two weeks in Malta and another two in Italy.

As I mentioned before, Lisa was finding it hard to concentrate on her studies so she decided to defer for a few months. She said she needed to go away to clear her head and travel overseas. Even though she was 23 years old, I wasn't very keen on her travelling alone especially in the state she was in, neither did her brother. Stephen really wasn't ready to travel yet, but he didn't want Lisa to go on her own either, so he decided to go backpacking with her. I felt a little better with them travelling together, and how thoughtful Stephen was to go with her.

Gary and I both thought it would be great idea that while they were travelling around Europe, we could all meet up in Malta. So it was organised and they would spend one week with us there. Gary and I thought we would surprise them and book two separate rooms for them in the same hotel which was at the waterfront at St Julian's as we knew they would be roughing it up in hostels. They were ever so thankful for it and it was so wonderful to share the country I was born in with my husband and children.

It was so emotional to be back in Malta; some in a good way and some not so good. The village where I was born seemed so small now and very different. After all, it had been over 25 years since I had visited Malta.

To my surprise, Gary liked it and the children loved it more. They both said they felt such a connection even though they were not born there. The house my parents built before we came to Australia was owned by my uncle now. We called them to see if we could visit and of course, they said it was fine.

When we got there I realised it was still the same. When I went in the front door, there was this huge open area with cars and a truck in it and I remembered that was where the animals were. They were doing some renovations there and had a great big hole in the middle of the open area; it was so dangerous. Obviously they didn't believe in occupational health and safety. No, not in Malta.

The small room where the kitchen was didn't have a door but a curtain to separate it from the lounge. It only had a few cupboards and a very old stove, which was better than what we had. I think it was the only improvement they did from the time we had it. The wrought iron stair case was still the same and had never been maintained; it was all scratched and dirty. There were the big bedrooms upstairs with single beds all around, and the cold, old-fashioned tiled room had a bath tub in it, still with no hot water. Then we went up the third level which was the roof. On it, was the clothes line and it was very unsafe as there was only a very low wall around the perimeter of the roof.

If any children went up there, they could easily fall onto the street. I tried very hard to take it all in and remember my uncle, my Mum's brother, sitting near the stairs looking so skinny, wrinkled and old. He was still working the land and spent a lot of his years in the hot sun. I'm so glad we got to see it again as I had always wanted to go back to my roots.

My Children

We also visited our local beach we went to as children called Lapsi. I would have loved to go swimming there but we just didn't have the time.

Stephen said he had to go somewhere and would be back later in the afternoon. I thought it was strange as he didn't know anyone in Malta and Lisa had a little smirk on her face. So when he came back that afternoon, he said he had something to show us. He pulled up his sleeve and got a tattoo of the Maltese cross done on the top of his arm. He told me he did the Maltese cross as he was proud of his heritage. I was surprised as he hadn't had any other tattoos done before.

We had a great time in Malta – especially with my children there. I have never forgotten that trip. Lisa and Stephen set off again to finish the rest of their holiday, and Gary and I left to start our tour of Italy. We got to see a lot of Italy and even visited one of Gary's friends who decided to go back to Italy and live. We had an amazing trip and eventually, headed home.

Lisa and Stephen infront of the old bus in Malta.

Stephen and Antonia on St Nicholas monument in Siggiewi, our old village.

My Children

Stephen, Antonia (Mum), Lisa and Gary in Malta.

One week after we arrived back in Australia, Lisa and Stephen returned home, it was nice to see them home safely. Lisa came back with a clearer head and decided to go back to studying, but she was missing her best friend and still grieving for her. She seemed to have withdrawn a little and after six years with her boyfriend, she decided to end the relationship. She was still very sad and angry all the time.

Her friend's case was all over the news for many years and it was so difficult to see it as I knew it was a terrible time for both Lisa and her friend's family. It broke my heart to see Lisa suffering like that. When something like that happens, it changes your whole perspective on life.

She got back into her PHD and only had six or so months left to finish it. When Lisa had a target she always met it.

Unfortunately mid-way through her PhD, her supervisor received an academic position at Brunel University in England. She had established good momentum developing biomechanical models with him and didn't want to start again. So, being the wanderlust and determined person she was, she decided to go to England to finish her PhD there. Thankfully, she had received a scholarship from the University of Sydney to do her studies, so was able to live frugally off of that.

I was very worried about her being on her own with no family support system. But the strong and determined person that she is, she went to England, put her head down and finished it over there.

She came back to Australia and graduated with her doctorate as Dr Lisa Bridgett. What an amazing job she did, too.

After finishing, she was soon employed by the university lecturing in her field. Not bad for a child who was supposed to be 'average'.

Chapter 17

Mum

Whilst all this was happening, we noticed Mum was very sad and always crying.

Doris, Salvina, Rita and I would visit her through the week and we all noticed that Mum was different. She was like that for quite a while. So I decided that we keep a journal of the things she would say and do during the time we were there.

She loved her garden and knitting, but she would go out to the garden for 10 minutes or so and then come back inside and start knitting. She would knit for 10 to 15 minutes and then go back in the garden. Then she would say I need to go to the shops, and we would take her and she would forget why she was at the shops.

Secrets of a Maltese Girl

My brother Nick was going through a divorce and asked Mum if he could live there until he bought another house to live in. He also noticed things were not right with Mum. He told us she would hide all the frying pans, pots and other things. When he asked Mum where they were, she would just stare blankly at him.

He would go looking for them around the house and find them in one of the bedrooms hidden in the wardrobe. At first, we thought she was being unreasonable or just got fed up with having people living in her house.

On my many visits, she would be sitting on her favourite chair knitting, and all of a sudden, I could see the tears roll down her cheek. It was such a sad thing to see. I've seen Mum cry many times before, but this type of crying was different. I could tell it was a cry of deep sadness.

I asked her what was wrong and she would start talking about her life when she was very young. She would go back as far as five years old, if not younger. She told me about the many times her mum asked her to do something, and when she didn't do it straight away, she would lash out on her.

One particular time, my grandmother was cooking soup and she asked Mum to stir it for her, but Mum didn't do it in time and it over boiled. My grandmother got really angry and she picked up the pot of soup and threw it over Mum. From my memory, I think Mum was around eight years of age. My grandmother obviously realised what she had done and took Mum to change from her wet clothes.

Mum

Mum was in a lot of pain and had to endure it all night as my grandmother didn't take her to the hospital until the next day. She warned Mum not to tell them how it happened. When they got to the hospital, she told them Mum pulled the pot over herself. They asked why she didn't bring Mum to the hospital as soon as it happened. She responded by saying she didn't think it was that bad.

Mum said she was in hospital for a long time. At least she got to rest in hospital as my grandmother always had her doing something. My grandfather just had to go along with it, as he knew that grandmother would be in a lot of trouble if they found out she did it.

There was another time when my grandmother was angry about something and she took it out on Mum. She was so badly beaten and had lots of very bad bruising and found it difficult to move. Normally, she would go with grandfather to help out in the fields, but when she didn't arrive, he was worried. He worked in the field all day and when he got home, he asked my grandmother where Mum was and she said she fell and wasn't feeling well.

When my grandfather saw her like that he knew that my grandmother had done this to her. He took her straight to hospital and when he got there, of course they asked him how this happened.

To cover up for my grandmother, he told them she fell in the street. They would have known the bruising was not from a fall as they had seen Mum in the hospital many times before. There were a lot of these incidents that had happened to Mum. She cried so much while she was telling me all these stories. Poor Mum held on to these sad stories for such a long time. And as sad as it was listening to her, I'm glad she got the opportunity to get them out. Mum couldn't remember what she did 10 minutes ago, but she certainly remembered the hard times.

She always had a lot of praise about her father. She would say he was a gentle man and he never laid a hand on them and had lots of patience. He had to be patient to be married to a woman like that. I don't remember my grandmother a great deal as they say a young child mainly remembers fond things about their grandparents, and there aren't too many fond memories of my grandmother.

My grandmother started suffering from dementia, which at the time I didn't know what it was. I remember she was always angry, and violent; she would scream so loud. I have seen her tied to her bed so she wouldn't run away or hurt anyone. I remember Mum and my grandfather spoon-feeding her and she was so skinny, but still had a lot of energy and fire in her. Grandmother died at the age of 86; one year before we migrated to Australia and Grandfather died exactly one year after we arrived in Australia at the age of 92.

As I mentioned earlier, we documented her behaviour and everything she said to us in an exercise book. Her behaviour grew stranger, so we decided to take her to her family doctor. When we told him what was happening, he thought that Mum was suffering from the beginning of dementia. We were all so busy with our own families and getting on with life in general, we didn't see it coming.

Before all this was happening with Mum, my two cousins decided to bring aunty (Mum's sister) to Australia to visit Mum and stay with us in our home. One morning, my aunty decided to brush her teeth,

Mum

so she got the big dish brush from the kitchen sink and started brushing. We laughed about it and thought it was very strange and later learnt that she too had the onset of dementia.

When they went back to Malta, she got worse and both cousins decided they would leave their jobs and look after her full time. She spent her time carrying a baby doll all day. She died many years later.

Mum's other sister was a nun and the church gave her permission to come to Australia to visit Mum. She also stayed with us in our home and strange things were happening with her, too. One particular time she got dressed and came out with her bra on the outside of her dress. When Mum saw her, she said, *"What you are doing? Go get dressed properly!"*

She just stared at Mum as I don't think she understood what Mum was saying to her. Mum had to go undress her and show her how to put her bra on under her dress. It was funny, but again, very sad.

My son Stephen was doing his confirmation whilst my aunty was visiting and she was invited to come to the celebration. When it came to receiving Holy Communion, she had a moment and wanted to receive Holy Communion the old-fashioned way.

Back then, we used to kneel in front of the altar and receive communion – where now, you walk up to the priest and receive communion in the palm of your hand. Well what did she do? She went up to the altar, knelt down and the priest had this strange look on his face but had no choice but to give her communion at the altar.

She did have her nun's clothes on, so hopefully he figured she was old school. Again, another sister with the onset of dementia. Three of my aunties which were Mum's sisters back in Malta died of dementia.

They did some tests on Mum and as far as her fitness went, she was very fit and strong. After all, she was still doing her own lawn at the age of 83. After the many doctors' visits, Mum was also diagnosed with dementia.

We continued to visit on a regular basis and my sister Colleen lived just across the main road and came to visit daily.

We noticed Mum's dementia was getting worse, so we decided to organise a meeting with our other siblings. My brothers didn't visit as often as the girls did, so they weren't there often enough to see the changes in Mum.

We called our oldest brother Fred to let him know what was going on with Mum and to contact our other brothers to organise a meeting to discuss Mum's situation. A day was set for us to meet, and most of us turned up but not all.

We all agreed that Mum couldn't be on her own as she was becoming a danger to herself. By that time, she was getting very forgetful and we were worried that she would go shopping and forget where she was and couldn't get back home. This happens often with people with dementia.

Mum

We decided there should be someone with her at all times. So it was suggested by one of the girls that since there were 13 children, surely we could have someone there every day and night.

Most siblings said they couldn't do it as they were still working and very busy. We were all busy with our families, but this was our mother and we had to do everything we could to look out for her.

My sister Doris wasn't working, Rita, Salvina and I had part time work and we still had children at home. Colleen was not working but said she had to look after her husband. So Salvina, Doris, Rita, my younger brother Nick and I took the responsibility to look after Mum.

We set up a roster and since three of us worked part time, it was decided that on the days we didn't work, we stayed over at Mum's for one day and one night, and on the alternative weeks, we would stay two nights as there were only three of us girls doing it. My younger brother had moved out into his own home but came to look after Mum over the weekend. It was working well for all of us.

It was interesting to see what she did most of the day while I was there looking after her. Mum had a dog which she loved and God bless her, in the evening, she would feed him and put him in the laundry to bed. Then she would wait 20 minutes or so and would take him out of the laundry and feed him again. She did this all the time, and I would sneak and take the food away from the dog. I told my sisters this and they also looked out for the dog.

During the day, she would go out into the garden to dig a hole to plant something, then she would come inside five minutes later, and the go back out and dig another hole. She kept doing this on and off for most of the day.

She would start knitting and do it for a few minutes, put it down and start again. She just couldn't stay still; it made me tired just to look at her. We had to have the side gates padlocked and hide the key as she would sneak out to visit my sister across a main road.

In the evenings, I would get her ready for her shower. She didn't know what to do, so I'd tell her to take her clothes off and put the shower on for her. I always had to stay with her and show her how to soap herself and had to watch her very carefully, as once she decided to turn the cold water tap off and nearly burnt herself with the hot water.

When she finished, she didn't know what to do next and I would get the towel and show her how to wipe herself. She had no idea what to do with her clothes either, so I had to dress her.

When it was time for bed, I would show her where her bedroom was and tuck her in. It was funny but sad at the same time as a few minutes later, she would come to my room and wanted to go out. I would take her back to her room and tell her she needed to stay there as this was her bed. It was just like looking after a baby.

She would wake up many times through the night, hence I didn't get much sleep or rest when I was with her. It was so sad and heartbreaking to see a women that was the strongest and most determined person I had ever known succumb to this, and now become so dependent on us looking after her. She was just like a young child again and it was up to us to care for her.

Mum

This went on for a little over three months and it was getting very difficult for all of us to look after her as she became more and more demanding. We were all tired and knew the time came for us to sort out some other care for Mum.

We scheduled another meeting and it was decided we would find a nursing home that catered for dementia patients. The research to find somewhere for her was left to Salvina, Rita and myself.

We looked everywhere and most of them were horrible places and so old and smelly. We felt Mum deserved the best. We found this brand new nursing home that was built by the Catholic Church where Mum attended and where we were all married. The only problem was that we had to buy into it. It had a dementia ward and a section for independent living. As it was brand new, there was a room for Mum with its own bathroom and coffee making facilities. All we had to do was to get her a bed and side table and her personal things.

This was a very expensive place to buy into. Mum didn't have that kind of money in the bank, but she did own her home, and a little money saved up, but not enough to buy into the nursing home. It was suggested by one of the siblings that since there were so many of us, we could all put a share and buy it until we are able to sell her home.

Everyone agreed, even though there were a couple of siblings that really couldn't afford it, but they managed and went ahead with it. The difficult task came to tell Mum that we were putting her into a nursing home. The thing with Mum having dementia was on the odd occasion, she could still be 'normal' to some extent.

Secrets of a Maltese Girl

Most of the siblings were able to meet up at mum's house, and Fred told her it was getting very hard for us to look after her at home, and she needed proper care, with doctors and nurses to look after her. He told her about us finding a really nice place built by the church where she attended. To our surprise, she understood what he was saying but she argued with him that she didn't want to go there, understandably.

We said to her she could take her own furniture, and there was also a garden, and we would visit every day. She started to cry and accused us of not caring, which I understood.

The time came to take her to the nursing home and it felt like we were abandoning her. The guilt and the sadness was enormous.

I found it so difficult to understand that out of 13 siblings, not one of us was prepared to continue to look after her. But I kept reasoning with myself that this is what we had to do. It wasn't a lack of respect or love, but a necessity. We all had children still living at home and most of us were still working.

She seemed to be doing okay in the nursing home and sometimes, she would know who we were and other times, she would have no idea. We worked out a visiting roster for some to visit in the morning and others in the afternoon. We always knew who visited and who didn't because we had to sign in and out every time we went to see her.

There were times when I went to visit she would ask me why I haven't visited her, and that nobody comes to see her. I would tell her that

Mum

I had visited yesterday and also the day before, but her mind kept lapsing all the time.

Not long after we moved her in the nursing home, my brother Frank died of cancer at the age of 56. We knew we had to tell her, even if she possibly wouldn't understand. So it was decided that the siblings would meet at the nursing home along with some of their spouses.

My oldest brother Fred was elected to give her the bad news. When he told her the news, I will never forget the look on her face and how she wailed and cried so much. To watch someone learn that their child had passed away was the saddest and most heartbreaking image. We were surprised that she understood what had happened.

A few months passed, and I could see she was declining very fast. She had a kettle in her room to make coffee and tea, and on one of the days I visited, I asked if she wanted a coffee. She nodded and when I went to fill up the kettle, it was full of coffee granules, and no water. I knew then that we would have to take the kettle out of her room as she was too confused to know how to use it or to make coffee.

She started to hide things again; all her spoons and cups would be in her wardrobe. I would find things that didn't belong to her and later found out that was part of her dementia.

Another time I visited, I noticed her bedspread was missing and I asked her where it was and she just stared at me. So I looked in her wardrobe and she had it rolled up so tight with a coat hanger wrapped around it. It was exactly how she used deliver the food for my father to the field – except they used rope around the cloth with the pot of food in it. But she compromised by using a wire coat hanger. I had a grin on my face but felt very sad that Mum's behaviour has come to this. Her mind must have been back to her youth and country of birth.

When it was time for me to leave, I would have to trick Mum by saying I'm going to get something or go to the toilet as she would start crying and wanted me to stay. It was getting more and more difficult for me to visit as I hated to see Mum upset like a child every time I had to leave her.

When she was at the nursing home for about nine months, Gary and I went to visit on a Saturday, she was sitting on a chair holding a teaspoon that she took from the kitchen. I noticed that she was looking at me strangely, and for some reason, I don't know why, I kept staring at her. All of a sudden, she started to shake and I realised she was having a seizure. I quickly wrapped my arms around her upper body whilst she was still on the chair so she wouldn't fall. I asked Gary to go and get a nurse, they called the doctor and he confirmed it was a seizure but couldn't explain why she had it. It was so frightening to see as I have never seen anyone have a seizure before.

She never had another seizure again. She started to wonder out of her room a lot and was very agitated – especially around three o'clock in the afternoon. She started to have falls and we couldn't understand why, until we found out they were medicating her. She would get out of bed and still be drowsy from the medication and fall.

She had bruises on her face and body all the time. Because she wasn't able to go to the dining room for her meals anymore, due to her falling all the time. They would bring them to her room, but there was no one to help her with her meals as they were always understaffed. She didn't know what to do, and we suspected what was happening so we started to visit just after meal time to see what was happening. Most of the time when we got there, the food was still on the tray, the tea lady would come and take the lot away. No one cared if she ate or not. That's why she was losing so much weight. We bought this to their attention and then they started to feed her.

They were having problems with some of the staff and Mum wasn't getting bathed regularly and her bathroom was always dirty and smelly. There were times when we had to clean it ourselves. The bins wouldn't be emptied for a whole week, and the towels weren't changed on a regular basis. We were paying big money for Mum to be there and be cared for the way she deserved.

Again, we expressed our concern but nothing improved, she was still being neglected. So we decided to take her out of there as soon as it was possible. We started looking for another nursing home. We searched everywhere, and it seemed the only way we could find her a place is if someone passed away, which was sad in itself.

One of the places we inquired at called us to say they had a place for her. This was not far from the other nursing home and was convenient for all the family to visit.

We moved her into it and she was only in there not even a week when we got a call from them to say that they could not keep her there. When we asked why, they said she snuck out of the building and they couldn't find her for hours. It was supposed to be a high care nursing home, but it seemed it wasn't secure enough for people who wandered out, like Mum.

We were beside ourselves as we had the daunting task of looking for another one. We called some of the places we inquired at before and one said there was a bed available, but it was a shared room with two other women. It was a clean place and again, not far away from the family. We went to check it out again and it certainly was for high care patients. We accepted the room and moved Mum in.

We continued to visit Mum at the nursing home and we could see that she was declining very fast. She couldn't recognise any of us and was bedridden and had to be fed soft foods as she could choke on solids.

She loved mangos and my sister Salvina would take some in to her, scoop it out with a spoon and feed her. She spent a total of three years in a nursing home and passed away at the age of 87, just four days before mine and Salvina's 50th birthday.

My biggest regret and sadness is out of 12 of us, not one of us was with her when she passed away.

After she passed, I remember thinking, and these were my exact words, *"What the hell was that all about? The poor women came into this world, had such a tough life growing up. Never had any fun, gave birth to all those children, the worries, the debts, and worked her butt off, for what?"*

That's when I made up my mind that I was going to try and enjoy my life while I still had good health.

Chapter 18

Travel Bug

My twin sister and I had a trip to New Zealand organised for our 50th birthday and were in two minds if we should go. We felt guilty about it, but we still went ahead with it and enjoyed ourselves. But Mum was always on my mind and in my heart.

When we got back from New Zealand, I had this very strong urge to go back to Malta. I just felt that I needed to connect with my birthplace again. I knew it had something to do with Mum's death. I mentioned to my sisters how I felt and strangely enough they also felt the same way. So it was decided that four of us girls would go to Malta together – no husbands, just us. So we proceeded to organise it and went ahead with it.

When we got to Malta, it was sad but lovely at the same time. Sad because of some of the not so good memories, but I felt elated at the same time as we are not the same poor people we were back then. We all grew up to be nurturing mothers, fathers, carers and amazing people, and are extremely comfortable with who we have become.

I couldn't believe how many people still recognised us. We went to our local beach, Lapsi. We visited our old house again, our beautiful church and some relatives. We ate lots of our traditional pastries, and it was so nice to reconnect again. Seeing Malta with my sisters was one of the most wonderful experiences we have ever shared. We had such an amazing time together, and lots of laughs too. The bond we formed between us was the best and I will never forget. It was a dream come true.

Doris, Salvina, Rita and Antonia in Malta having fun.

Rita, Doris, Antonia and Salvina at a bakery in Malta.

It was time to go back home and settle into life again, Gary and I decided to sell our home and build a new one. We bought a block of land to build our new home on. In the meantime, Gary started to build his son's house on weekends, and because it took such a long time building it, it took its toll on Gary. He had to drive such a long way there, and after a hard day's work, he had to drive back home again. I was always worried about him driving home when he already was so exhausted

He was always helping one person or another, with just a thanks, and he could never say no to anyone. He is one of the kindest man I know, and unfortunately, many times, he was taken advantage off.

So, we decided to engage a company to build our home. We sold our principle home and lived in our holiday home at the Central Coast while it was being built. Just as we sold our home, we go some bad news that Gary was diagnosed with cancer, and we weren't sure if we should go ahead and build.

He had his big operation and thank God, he is now cancer-free. So we went ahead and started building our beautiful home that we live in today.

Chapter 19

Becoming a Grandmother

After our big scare and before grandchildren came along, we decided to do a little more travel. This time, we wanted to visit Canada. I have visited Canada before with the company I worked for and loved it so much. We asked my twin sister Salvina and her husband if they also wanted to come. They loved the idea and agreed, then my sister Rita and her husband expressed they wanted to go too. So we asked my other sister Doris if she would like to come as her husband had just passed away and it would be good for her to come with us. All agreed and we start to organise the trip.

We decided that we were going to go all out and visit Alaska and do the Rocky Mountaineer. The time came to leave for Canada and we were so excited to be travelling together again. Especially because my sister Doris would be having her 60th birthday while we were there.

Just before we were due to go, my daughter Lisa asked if we could go out for brunch. We had our food and she gave me a package, and I just thought it was something for the trip. Lo and behold, she presented me with a dummy. I couldn't believe it; she was telling me that she was pregnant.

I was so elated and surprised at the same time. I was finally becoming a grandmother. It was decided that we not tell anyone until she reached three months gestation. It was so difficult to keep a secret like that while I was holidaying with my sisters. I wanted to tell them so badly. We had the most wonderful trip in Canada and saw so many beautiful places. I would have to say it was one of the most memorable holidays I've had as far as beauty goes.

I was so glad that we decided to do this trip as I knew when babies came along, I would be needed to help out. The time came to tell the family and a few family members were a bit taken back because she was not married to her partner, but who cares? I certainly didn't. I was just happy I was finally becoming a grandmother and was looking so forward to the baby's arrival.

Whilst all this was happening, our new house was being built and it took longer than they said it would, of course. I was still working three days a week and Gary by then had retired and went back as a consultant for the same company three days a week.

Becoming a Grandmother

We were hoping to move into our new home before Christmas, but that didn't happen. I was eager to move as I didn't want to be too far from Lisa when she had the baby.

We moved into our new home in February. And Lisa gave birth to a beautiful daughter Sofia at the beginning of May. I was over the moon and couldn't wait to hold her. Lisa left hospital and got into motherhood. I would go there and help out as much as I could as Lisa was fairly nervous. She went through the norm with breastfeeding and lots of sleepless nights.

She wanted to go back to work three days a week when Sofia was six months old. I said I would look after her two days and my ex-husband would look after her for one day, as he was very capable. Of course, I always had everything prepared for Sofia when her grandfather came to look after her the next day.

My workplace was a one-hour drive from our new house and I hated the drive, as I would be so tired when I got home. So Gary and I discussed my retirement and it was decided that I would retire at the age of 60. It made it a lot easier and less stressful when I looked after Sofia.

When Sofia was around 17 months old, we had our regular family get together with my sisters, and my ex-husband was also there, as he was always welcomed to our get together – especially when our children and Sofia was there.

When most of the family members left, she asked her father to stick around. This time, Lisa and her partner had two wrapped up boxes.

Secrets of a Maltese Girl

She gave one to each of us, we opened them up and inside were two lots of booties, two dummies and two little ducks. I knew straight away what they were trying to tell us. But her father didn't work it out. You guessed it, she was telling us she was pregnant with twins.

I couldn't believe it, but I was not surprised as we have a history of twins in our family. Unfortunately, she lost one at two months and had a few issues for the rest of the pregnancy. Thank God she gave birth to a healthy, gorgeous baby boy named Isaac in early July. What a surprise that was; he was born with jet-black, spiky hair.

Lisa expressed that she wanted to go into a different line of work when Isaac was four months old, as she knew she had to be flexible when the children went to school. She wanted to try it for two days a week. I told her that I would look after Isaac while she explored her new venture. She was all in and started mortgage broking, working for someone else for two years.

She loved it so much and was doing extremely well, so she decided to go solo and started her own company. It took a lot of guts for her to do that, as she still had a young family and a mortgage to pay. But she always had my full support.

Cracks started to show in the relationship with her partner when the children were only nearly three and Isaac was just a baby. As a mother, I knew that one day this would happen. I was prepared but not happy about it, and I knew we were in for a very difficult time.

She decided to break up with him as she didn't want the children to feel or see the animosity that was being created, like it was in her parents' marriage. She lived an hour's drive from us, and it was decided that she move closer to our home to make it easier when she needed us to help out. It was a very difficult time for all of us; it's not what I wanted for her or for Sofia and Isaac.

They both decided to share custody of the children. Their father loves them dearly and he always expressed that to them, so it was a bonus to know both their parents expressed so much love to them. I made sure they didn't miss out on anything. I was always cooking food for them as Lisa was busy enough with her work.

I bought them nice clothes and shoes, took them to libraries for reading and dance time. I took a course in cake decorating to make sure they always had beautiful birthday cakes, and sometimes they would ask for the impossible, but I try to please them the best I can. They became my focus and were now a very big part of mine and Gary's life. They are wonderful children and very loving towards Gary and I. There is always a cuddle waiting for us, and, an I love you.

The kids on one of their skiing holidays.

Becoming a Grandmother

Isaac, Antonia (me) and Sofia at The Entrance.

Sofia and Isaac at her Holy Communion.

Becoming a Grandmother

Antonia, Sofia, Lisa and Isaac.

Sofia and Lisa (mum)

Stephen and Isaac at Isaac's birthday celebration.

Sofia and Nanna (me).

Becoming a Grandmother

Sofia and Isaac on his birthday.

Time flies and they are both at school now. My daughter Lisa decided to buy her own home as she wanted a yard for the kids. She needed to buy in an area not far from her ex-partner or the school they attended as it was important both of them with drop-offs and pick-ups.

The task of finding a home she liked was so daunting, as the properties there were extremely expensive – not to mention she was very fussy. She found this particular home and asked me to go have a look at it. At first I thought, *"Oh my god what is she thinking? It's a knock down!"*

My husband couldn't come for some reason, so I called him and told him how old it was. It had huge trees everywhere and you could hardly see the house from the overgrown shrubs. But she wanted this house as it was only a few kilometres from the city and had a reasonable size yard for that area.

So, my husband and I went to look at it again to see what we can do with it. It had beautiful original stained-glass windows and I could see why she fell in love with it. I loved old houses too, but this one was a lot of work. Gary and I did a few home renovations we bought for investments and because he was a builder by trade, he had a lot of knowledge.

We played around with some ideas and it was decided that if she bought it, we would gut it all out. So she bought the house and as soon as it settled, it was all systems go. The house was completely gutted out inside to the bare frame.

In the meantime, Lisa was getting pricing for all sorts of material and this particular guy came to quote her for something, but kept coming around all the time. Gary and I queried why this guy was hanging around so much.

Our suspicions were right as they had started a friendship and fallen in love. He was very knowledgeable in the building game and very helpful in organising trades and helping out with some of the renovation. My son Stephen did some of the electrical and cabling for the internet in between traveling for his work. I did lots of painting and puttying nail holes and sanding and gardening.

By the time it was finished, it looked like a brand new home. Gary built a large carport for her car as the garage was demolished to make room for a brand new office come studio for her to work in – complete with a toilet, shower, laundry and kitchen. So now she has the luxury of working from home and having the flexibility to work whenever she wants. Gary worked really hard to get the house finished quickly as she was paying rent and a second mortgage.

She had a lot of guts to do it on her own again. But she is her mother's daughter and we never say never. It was hard work for all of us – her included, as she had all that happening around her and was trying to run a business at the same time. She was fortunate to have Gary do it for her, and he did it from the goodness of his heart, and out of respect for me.

After it was all finished, I said to Gary, *"That's it, no more renovating houses. We're not getting any younger!"*

But when we saw the final product, it was all worth it. Especially to see her so happy and the children having a yard to play in. She moved in two and a half months after she bought it.

As a thank you for doing all the work for her, she surprised us with a week away at the Yarra Valley. We had a gorgeous cabin and visited many wineries there and we did a lot of relaxing. Both my children always did something special for us every time we helped them, so it was always nice to be appreciated.

I still help out on Monday and Tuesday, pick the children up from school, take them to their after school activities, help them with their homework and cook dinner for them. Sometimes, if Stephen is around and not travelling, he comes over to her place to join us for dinner as he lives 15 minutes away from her.

Gary and I managed to do more travels, as we would try not to let our responsibilities with the children get in our way. There are times where we go away for a few weeks, and we try and plan it when Sofia and Isaac are with their dad, so Lisa would only have to do school pick up for a few days.

Chapter 20

Doris' Final Battle

Doris was in remission for 20 years. But by mid-2023, she started to feel unwell. She battled cancer that many times, she knew the signs. The oncologist who treated her before had retired, and it was time to find a new one. This time around, it wasn't non-Hodgkin's lymphoma, but lung and breast cancer.

The battle was on again for Doris and she told me that this time, she didn't want to have chemotherapy as she knew how sick she would get and didn't want to go through it again. Who could blame her? Poor thing.

She also expressed this to her daughter, but after much discussion, she decided to have treatment. She had two choices of treatment. One was to have intravenous chemotherapy and the other was immunotherapy which would cost her over AUD$4,000 per month. It was decided to go for the immunotherapy, as we didn't want her to be prodded with so many needles and having to spend endless hours in hospital. She was able to have her treatment at home.

Doris started her treatment and she seemed to handle it quite well at first. We were very surprised as she didn't seem to have too many side effects. But three months into it, she started to lose weight and was feeling very tired all the time.

We were grateful that she lived in an over-55 retirement village, as she made many friends and they would keep an eye on her. Many times her daughter would get a call from Doris' friend to say Doris was not doing well and to call an ambulance. They would do blood test after blood test and it was so very sad and awful to see. As she had so many rounds of chemotherapy in the past, her veins were not good at all, and she would be in so much pain when they tried to draw blood from her; she would have so many bruises.

My sister Salvina and I would often have her over to our place for the day and sometimes, the night too. On this particular day when she was at my place, she went to the toilet and was in there for a very long time. I kept checking and asking if she was okay. After a while she didn't respond, so I opened the door and she was unresponsive whilst on the toilet. You can imagine the fright I got when I saw her like that.

I called an ambulance straight away and thank God it only took the paramedics 15 minutes to get to my place. They couldn't wake her up and I thought this was it. I called her daughter, and my sister and I met them at the hospital.

Doris' Final Battle

They worked on her, and she woke up for a while, and then all of a sudden, she started to convulse. They asked us to leave the room and every doctor and nurse that was available rushed to her room. Again, we thought we lost her that day, but she came through. She wasn't ready to go yet.

She was released from hospital but ended up in intensive care a few days later. They said to us there was nothing more they could do for her and she only had 24 to 48 hours left to live. We were told to inform family members to say their goodbyes. We all took turns going into her room to spend time with her and say our goodbyes. We both cried and cried and she was very open to the knowledge of not making it out of hospital. I assured her we would be there for her daughter and grandchildren as she was very worried about how they would cope.

She was in intensive care for four days, and to the doctor's surprise, she started to improve. What a fighter she was. The doctors came to the conclusion that the medication she was on was causing all this to happen, so Doris decided she no longer wanted treatment as she had no quality of life. We realised she couldn't live on her own any longer, even though she had friends in the village that would check in on her.

We spoke to Doris about our concerns of her living alone and she agreed that she didn't want to go home and be on her own. So we discussed the option of palliative care, as the hospital she was in had a palliative care unit. But they couldn't admit her because she improved and wasn't completely bedridden. They suggested home care, but it was only a few hours a day and she needed someone with her all the time. So it was decided that we look for a nursing home for her as she would have around the clock care.

Secrets of a Maltese Girl

Her daughter found a beautiful new nursing home that had just been built and only five minutes' drive from where she lived, but unfortunately for us, it was over an hour's drive. We moved her in there and tried to make it as much like home as we possibly could. The dreaded job of selling her home, and emptying it begun. She was so house proud and to have to sell her furniture and other belongings was so sad and awful to see.

She seemed to be happy at the nursing home and the staff were wonderful, who looked after her very well. The siblings would visit her as often as they could and my twin sister and I would visit her weekly and speak on the phone daily. We would take her shopping and also take her some Maltese food she was familiar with.

She wasn't able to walk too far without being breathless. We all dreaded the worst every time we visited. Doris was 69 years old at the time.

I said to her on one of my visits, *"You want to hang around for your 70th birthday, don't you?"*

And she said, *"Yes."*

I replied, *"Okay, we better start planning your 70th birthday party then!"*

So I called her daughter when I got home and she was already on it. Her surprise birthday party was planned a week before her birthday as on the day of her birthday was Father's day.

Doris' Final Battle

Her daughter told her they were taking her out to lunch and when they arrived, she was so surprised and excited to see everybody there. All the siblings were there, along with some of our children and grandchildren and her friends from the village. We all had a wonderful time and lots of family photos were taken with Doris, as we all knew this was our last opportunity.

I continued to visit Doris regularly on a Wednesday, and on this visit, Doris was really down and crying. She said to me, *"Why has God done this to me? I have suffered so much for so long. I don't want to live like this anymore."*

My heart just broke for her and for a little while, I was speechless and all I could do was just hold her hands and sit with her. She settled down after a long while and said, *"I feel like eating some fish. Can you take me to the shops?"*

I said, *"Yes, of course!"*

When we got there, I bought her some fish – which was awful. We walked for just a few minutes as she couldn't walk long. Then she said I feel like a Chico roll, so I went a got one for her and she devoured it. She would often get Chico rolls. Doris still had a pretty good appetite for someone who was very sick. I asked her if she also wanted a cappuccino as she was always complaining the coffee at the nursing home as *"not nice and always cold."*

We had our coffee and it was so good to see her a little happier. I took her back to the nursing home and stayed with her for a little while longer. It was time for me to go home as I had a long drive and didn't want to get stuck in the school pick up traffic. I gave her a kiss, told her I loved her, and said, *"See you next Wednesday."*

My sisters Salvina and Rita visited Doris the next week on Tuesday. She wasn't feeling well and the doctor came while they were there and was concerned that her heart was beating very fast. It was decided that she needed to go to hospital. The ambulance came an hour later, and the paramedic asked if there was to be any intervention should she need it. Salvina's response was, *"No, Doris doesn't want to die in hospital."*

Salvina and Rita went downstairs whilst Doris was being wheeled out of the nursing home and put into the ambulance. Before they closed the door, Salvina called out to Doris that she loved her and that was the last time she saw her alive. That night, the hospital rang her daughter to come and pick her up and take her back to the nursing home. On the way home, she told her daughter she felt like having pizza. So she got her some pizza and drove to the nursing home.

At 10:30am the next morning, Salvina called Doris to see how she was and she told her, *"I've had a good breakfast and am feeling okay."*

I would normally visit on Wednesday, but that week, I could only visit Doris on Thursday. But on Wednesday, around 12:30pm in the afternoon, I got a call from my sister Salvina to say Doris had just passed away. I knew it would happen sooner or later, but I didn't want to believe it. My biggest regret is that I wasn't with her when she died as I should have been there that day.

Doris' Final Battle

Salvina and I rushed to the nursing home and stayed with Doris for hours, until they had to take her away. I still couldn't believe she died, even though I knew it was near.

I miss Doris so much and think about her every day; she is at peace now and she will never be forgotten.

Growing up in a large family was incredibly challenging. Meeting all our needs seemed impossible, akin to surviving as a weed with minimal nurturing from our busy parents, who were focused on providing for us.

Both of my parents had tough lives themselves and while I understand their struggles, our upbringing was equally difficult.

Despite these hardships, I believe we thrived. Each of us found our own path to success, driven by the belief that nothing is beyond reach if pursued with determination. I can honestly say that all the siblings have done extremely well and established very successful businesses' despite their lack of education.

However we prioritised education and support for our children, who have gone on to achieve remarkable things. Among them are doctors, lawyers, medical researchers, medical scientists, electrical engineers, and many successful business owners.

Malta is the country of my birth, and it made me the person I am today: Resilient, hardworking, caring and nurturing. I was naturalised as an Australian many moons ago. And Australia is my home now and has been for nearly 60 years.

Secrets of a Maltese Girl

I would never have achieved all that I have if my brother Fred hadn't picked up that newspaper while sitting on the church steps (after being kicked out of the local pub) and saw the advertisement on immigration to Australia... Then convincing my parents to migrate to this wonderful country we live in.

Don't get me wrong – I had to work very hard to achieve all that I have. My husband and I have travelled to many different countries, and I could not imagine living anywhere else, but in this beautiful country of ours, Australia.

Doris.

Doris' Final Battle

Doris at the nail salon.

All of the family in one photo. Top row: Paul (Dad), Philippa (Mum), Colleen, Fred, Frank, Greg and George; Middle row: Manual, Mario, Joe, Doris, Antonia and Salvina; Bottom row: Nickholas and Rita.

All of the sibings at Doris' 70th birthday – our last family photo taken two months before Doris passed away. Top row: Fred, Rita, Joe, Nick and Mario. Bottom row: Greg, Colleen, Antonia, Salvina, George, Manaul and Doris.

One of many cruises with Salvina, Antonia, Doris and Rita.

Celebrating Gary's birthday with Stephen, Antonia, Lisa, Sofia, Gary and Isaac.

Lisa and Antonia.

Antonia and Stephen on Mothers Day.

Sofia's 9th birthday with Poppy, Grandpa and Nanna (me).

Gary and Antonia at her 69th birthday.

Salvina and Antonia in Japan.

Gary and Antonia in Croatia.

Valletta, The Capital City of Malta. 2024

**Antonia and Husband Gary in Malta 2024.
Just as her book was completed.**

About the Author

People describe me as selfless, with endless love for those around me. My children and grandchildren are the centre of my world and I cherish every moment with them.

Watching my grandchildren play sports and engage in activities that bring them joy fills my heart with happiness. Spending time with my children and enjoying the simple pleasures of life brings me immense contentment.

I find joy in yoga and morning walks in the crisp morning air, embracing the tranquillity and promise of each new day. Retreating to our holiday house with my husband, Gary, allows me to relax and enjoy the serenity and beauty of nature.

Sharing nice dinners with family and good friends is a source of great pleasure, as I treasure the warmth, laughter, and connection these moments bring.

I have a passion for travel, revelling in the opportunity to see new places, meet new people, and experience diverse cultures. These adventures enrich my life and broaden my perspective, making each journey a cherished memory. I'm partial to a good game of *Rummikub* with my nearest and dearests, and I find peace and satisfaction in gardening, nurturing plants, and watching them thrive.

Writing this book has been a deeply personal journey, helping me find peace with my past while documenting it for future generations. It is my hope that my children and their children will one day read this book and gain a profound understanding of the roots from which they came, connecting them to their heritage and the rich history of our family.

Acknowledgements

To my amazing children, Lisa and Stephen, your unwavering support and love have been my anchor throughout this journey. This book is a testament to the pride I feel in being your mother. I hope I have made you proud of me as I am of you.

To my twin sister Salvina, your deep understanding and help in navigating our rich family history in Malta and Australia have been invaluable. Your companionship and insights have helped me find further meaning to my story.

To my husband Gary, who stands by me unconditionally. Thank you for your endless support, love, and understanding. Your patience during the countless hours I spent in the office, has been a true testament to your unwavering commitment and love.

Notes